The Reign
of
Napoleon III

THE REIGN OF NAPOLEON III

BRISON D. GOOCH
University of Connecticut

RAND McNALLY & COMPANY · **Chicago**

INITIAL BOOKS IN
THE RAND McNALLY EUROPEAN HISTORY SERIES
George L. Mosse, advisory editor

GEORGE FASEL, Europe in Upheaval: The Revolutions of 1848
BRISON D. GOOCH, The Reign of Napoleon III
HANS J. HILLERBRAND, Men and Ideas in the Sixteenth Century
BARBARA JELAVICH, The Habsburg Empire in European Affairs,
    1814–1918
HARRY J. MAGOULIAS, Byzantium: Emperor, Church and the West
JOHN B. WOLF, Toward a European Balance of Power

Editor's Preface

It used to be thought that the sole object of history was to discover and set forth the facts. When the *English Historical Review* was founded it recommended such a procedure, for through it one "can usually escape the risk of giving offense." While much of this tradition has remained active in the teaching and writing of history, it has led, in turn, to a sharp reaction against such timidity and narrowness. History became a branch of philosophy or of the social sciences, and scholarship was in danger of being displaced by the search for general laws that might govern the development of all mankind. There is a hunger for history abroad in the land, but many of those who want to know about the past are rightly dissatisfied with arid narrations of fact (and turn to the historical novel instead), while others are bewildered by abstruse generalizations that seem to ignore the particular for the universal.

The books in the Rand McNally European History Series do not place themselves in either of these traditions. Instead, they recognize both the importance of accurate and detailed scholarship and the obligation to place such scholarship within a meaningful historical setting. They do not shun general ideas and assumptions; they test them in the crucible of research. This combination is always exciting, because it penetrates historical development; and this development, in each of its stages, illuminates a new dimension of mankind. A prominent historian once wrote, "What man is, only history tells."

Here "what man is" is told by scholars who have researched and reflected upon a significant period of history. They have taken this opportunity to present their conclusions in a manner that will attract and stimulate those who long for a lively account of the past. All of the authors in this series are specialists presenting their original insights, making it possible for all those interested in history to partake of their work.

George L. Mosse, *advisory editor*
Rand McNally European History Series

Preface

This book hopes to present a view of Louis Napoleon (Napoleon III) that fairly recognizes the legitimate claims of both his critics and defenders during the past hundred years. The Emperor and his Empire are virtually indistinguishable, so that Napoleon III's story is very much France's story for more than two decades. Because this supremely political figure was also strongly motivated by social issues, our account accordingly emphasizes political and social developments in France, with less attention given to other aspects of the nation's life. Virtually every major topic touched on in our narrative has been the subject of a book-length study. Consequently, detailed chronological analyses have been sacrificed in this book in favor of a general overview, which itself represents an interpretive weighing of the record left by Napoleon III and his Empire. A nation such as France in the middle of the nineteenth century, with problems stemming from a welter of conflicting political ambitions, involvement in foreign wars and a remarkably expanding economy, may well have some hints for our own day. In addition, a diligent reader may discover that Louis Napoleon was a person intrinsically worth knowing.

BRISON D. GOOCH

February, 1969
Norman, Oklahoma

Contents

Chapter 1

Introduction

In 1839 Louis Napoleon Bonaparte was a dapper, thirty-one-year-old pretender, busily plotting his second amateurish and ill-fated coup. He was also writing *Napoleonic Ideas,* a popular, propagandistic blending of fact and fantasy in which he observed that Napoleon Bonaparte "had closed the gulf of revolutions" that the statesmen of Vienna in "overthrowing him, have reopened." With reference to the Enlightenment and the French Revolution, he claimed that Napoleon was "the only man able to mediate between two ages." If these comments were at all appropriate for Napoleon Bonaparte, they were to prove equally valid for their author, the future Napoleon III.

While deliberately making the most of his uncle's place in history, Louis was unwittingly writing a factual prelude to his own position in the nineteenth century. He assumed power as President of the Second French Republic in December, 1848, barely six months after the bloody June Days; four years later he converted the Republic into a new Napoleonic empire. He claimed that his imperial system brought stability and order to France and rested on the support of the masses rather than on armed force or a propertied, titled elite. After his fall in 1870, Frenchmen again zestfully killed one another in a savage replaying of urban violence.

The humiliating military defeat that ended the Second Empire tended to obscure its solid achievements, but later decades recognized the reign of Napoleon III as a period of profound change. Material progress was both real and apparent as Europe moved closer to the twentieth century. Since the regime had accepted the new without an outright rejection of the old, it appeared to be oriented toward the future while also looking backward. This divergence was the basic nature of the Empire and its leadership. As a consequence one historian has been able to argue cogently that the Emperor was out of step with his age, since so many of his ideas and attitudes reflect a twentieth-century orientation; yet with as much logic another scholar has maintained that Napoleon's problem was that while he lived and acted in the nineteenth century, his frustrations resulted from trying to apply the best of eighteenth-century concepts.

The Second Empire was a particularly transitional period. In those two decades, from 1850 to 1870, there were attempts to resolve the problems of authority, progress and social justice—issues that plagued much of Europe for the whole century. Midway between 1789 and 1918, the Empire was an interesting attempt to bring the two ages together. Such may be the view of the historian who is looking back over the rest of the century. However, the men of the 1850's and '60's played out their roles without knowing what the future was to hold; they saw only how they stood in relation to the past. And what of the past did they see?

From the experience of the French Revolution they saw a great unleashing of energy and a brutal example of what revolution really meant. Radicals were heartened by the birth of concepts of social equality and republicanism, while conservatives shuddered at the horrible events attending the breakup of a class-structured society. The Revolution seemed an entity in itself, to be feared and suspected behind every riot or hint of civic disturbance.

Napoleon Bonaparte appeared as the moderator of revolutionary excesses. His greatest failing was that his egocentric leadership of France became synonymous with an imperialistic order. Thus his domestic successes in promoting administrative and religious stability, creating a new nobility and consolidating a vast body of legal practice and law were all overbalanced by his aggressive and imperialistic foreign policy.

With the fall of Napoleon I, both France and Europe assumed a posture of aristocratic conservatism, making as little concession as possible to the revolutionary tide that had swept over most of the continent. Louis XVIII represented a tired acceptance of a modicum of change; but under his successor, Charles X, the spirit of reaction was dominant at court. At the same time the middle class in France was growing as business expanded. More and more, influential people were coming to expect a government that was at least congenial to the basic principles of liberalism. Charles X's ultra-royalism alienated even moderate liberals, who applauded his downfall. It was, perhaps, not so much his authoritarianism as his insistence on the forms and attitudes of the *ancien régime*, an age that had exhausted its credit in France by 1789. Charles X simply refused to recognize that after the Revolution and Napoleon, a return to a pre-1789 type of monarchy was impossible.

The next regime, that of Louis Philippe, was one to hearten the business classes. On the surface it was liberal and appeared to recognize the new elements in society. There was a reasonable tie with the past in that the King was of the Orleans family, related to the Bourbons but not too closely. Besides this semblance of legitimacy, the King's father, Philippe Egalité, had been a revolutionary. Equally important, Louis Philippe was acutely interested in the expansion of commerce and manufacturing, making him a seemingly apt choice after Charles X. However, as his reign progressed this monarch too became authoritarian and conservative. After 1840 his regime was corrupt as well. This, combined with a foreign policy that appeared to sacrifice national honor for peace and profits, finally led to his fall, and, like Charles X, he fled into exile in England.

1848 was the year of revolutions. Even the venerable Metternich fell from power as autocracy and authoritarianism were challenged in much of Europe. In Paris a complex combination of forces was at work. Louis Philippe's growing authoritarianism had alienated some people; others genuinely wanted a republic. Still others represented a new factor in society, an urban proletariat; and it may be that Louis Philippe's main error was that while he was sympathetic to the interests of an expanding class of business leaders, he paid inadequate attention to the workers. Missing in early 1848 were any signs of substantial support for a Bonaparte; yet by the end of the year Louis Napoleon was the nation's president.

In Paris in 1848 liberalism, republicanism, socialism and nationalism were intertwined in feverish efforts to devise an effective government to replace that of Louis Philippe. After much debate and political maneuvering between republicans and socialists, the decision-making process seemed to falter, and the republicans turned the army against their opponents. The slaughter of the June Days (1,500 dead in three days) revealed anew the failure of successive regimes since 1789 to reconcile the interests of different elements in the population. Clearly the constructive aspects of the 1789 revolution and the virtues of the *ancien régime* had not yet been adequately blended to handle a society undergoing rapid social change, with business expanding and both businessmen and urban workers becoming more abundant. Louis Napoleon's role in history is to be seen as yet another attempt to reconcile these divergent elements. Like his uncle, he "closed the gulf of revolutions"; he provided stability, finely balancing authority and democracy while allowing and supervising extensive industrial and social change. After his fall the "gulf" reopened and the world again caught sight of the savagery which had been suppressed for over two decades.

Between 1850 and 1870 France played an important role in the vast changes that occurred in Europe and abroad. Napoleon III was crucially involved in the boundary readjustments that by 1870 defined a new German Empire, a unified Italy and a Rumanian state. There was marked growth of industry, especially in Germany; in transportation, rail lines were being feverishly built all over western and central Europe, often with French finance and technicians. French technology built the Suez Canal, opening a new era in water communication with the Far East, where the arms of Napoleon III had reclaimed a French foothold all but lost in the eighteenth century. French foreign policy, however, was not uniformly successful as, for example, in Mexico where the French-sponsored emperor, Maximilian, was executed. Closer to home, Napoleonic designs on Belgium and Luxembourg caused suspicion and apprehension.

By 1870 the pace of change had quickened. The world was smaller and news was traveling faster. The telegraph wire had brought almost instant communication between the capitals of Europe and threatened to make messenger boys out of generals and diplomats alike. Though Napoleon's empire was not to survive the whirlwind of nationalism in central Europe, still it had shown a remarkable economic vitality at home, had stimulated enormous political and economic change abroad and was itself an interesting attempt to balance the various disruptive forces in France. Many historians regard its fall as really beginning in 1859 with the war in Italy. Over a decade later, however, the imperial system which Napoleon III had finally devised was strong enough to be ratified by an impressive vote at the polls, proving that the Empire was widely approved in France and that the Emperor was amazingly popular only a few short months before the military disaster signalling the end of the regime.

Chapter 2

The Nature of the Leader

Louis Napoleon and His Family

Napoleon III was born in Paris on April 20, 1808, and christened Charles Louis Napoleon Bonaparte. His mother was Hortense Beauharnais, a daughter of Josephine and a stepdaughter to Napoleon. His father was Louis Bonaparte, the brother of Napoleon and King of Holland. There were two other legal sons of the union of Hortense and Louis; but by 1835, the only one surviving was the future emperor, who was known before he came to power as Louis Napoleon—or, as he insisted, Prince Louis Napoleon.

The marriage of Hortense and the younger brother of Napoleon Bonaparte had been stormy. At one point Hortense accepted a natural son of Talleyrand as a lover and gave birth to Charles Auguste Joseph Demorny, later known as the Duc de Morny, an important figure in French business and political circles by the 1840's. The paternity of Louis Napoleon is itself shrouded, but most scholars concede that while the evidence is intriguing, it is also inconclusive and that in all probability his father was indeed the brother of Napoleon. At any rate, his birth was attended by fanfare and cannon-firing throughout French-controlled Europe, as he was a publicly acknowledged prince.

By the mid-1830's this prince was conducting himself as though he were the logical Bonapartist pretender. Two decades had passed since Waterloo, however, and few people took his claims seriously. Others of the family had, by then, reconciled themselves to the loss of power. Napoleon's father, Carlo, had died in 1785, but his mother, Letitia, lived until 1836. Of his sisters, Elisa died in 1820, Pauline in 1825 and Caroline in 1839. The Emperor's brothers lived a bit longer, Lucien dying in 1840, Joseph in 1844, Louis in 1846, while Jerome survived until 1860 and witnessed the Bonapartist restoration. No serious attempt to regain power was made by any of these brothers or sisters of Napoleon. It is interesting that while Louis Napoleon was putting himself forth as the pretender, his father and grandmother were yet alive, as well as three uncles and an aunt, all obviously closer than he to the great Emperor.

Another possible Bonapartist candidate for the throne of France was Napoleon's legal son, the King of Rome at birth, who lived out his life in rather splendid captivity at Schönbrunn, carrying the title of the Duke of Reichstadt. He was the generally recognized successor to the Emperor, but he died in 1832, the end of any direct line from Napoleon. Spain's ex-king Joseph then was the nominal head of the family but did not plot a return to power. The inactivity of Napoleon's brothers and sisters left the way open for members of the next generation. By the mid-1830's Louis was the oldest and the only one who at birth had been heralded as a prince throughout the Empire. He was also the most assertive and, through his writing and activities, managed to become publicly recognized as the leading Bonapartist claimant.

Within the family there was only one important dissenter to Louis as the pretender to Bonapartist power. He was Prince Napoleon (Joseph Charles Paul) Bonaparte, born in 1822, the son of Jerome, but his political ambitions seemed thwarted by chance. By the time this prince had acquired his ambitions, Louis Napoleon, who was older, had made his mark. Prince Napoleon was openly jealous and hostile toward his cousin Louis, who recognized him as a source of potential trouble and, when in power, patiently tried to soothe his vanity. Such efforts were barely appreciated as the Prince freely criticized government programs. Politically far to the left, he kept company with demagogic radicals and had a reputation for immorality. He even called attention to the doubts about Louis' paternity and openly referred to his cousin as "not even a member of the family." If this were true, of course, then the rise to power of

Prince Louis Napoleon was all the more phenomenal.

The pretender to Bonapartist power was a frail and unprepossessing figure. Like his father, he was moody and reflective and seemed utterly to lack the dynamism and dramatic fire associated with Napoleon. Indeed, he bore less physical resemblance to his uncle than did several others in that famous clan. He had a far less angular face, a much larger nose, a wide but sharply receding forehead, and he sported a moustache and beard. Both Jerome's son, Prince Napoleon, and daughter Mathilde strikingly resembled their uncle. Louis appeared so placid, slow-moving and deliberate that at first glance it was difficult to take his claims seriously. The look of his eyes suggested a mind far away and uninvolved in the events of the present. Some men took this, to their ultimate regret, as an indication of slow or mediocre thought processes, even incompetence. In later life his mien suggested to some that of a German professor of philology. A quiet, genial man, he looked as though he belonged in a book-lined study. He could hardly be imagined as the leader of such an emotionally charged movement as Bonapartism.

Through a phenomenal career, Napoleon Bonaparte had set the stage for a successor and at Saint-Helena had even indicated the lines by which a Bonapartist propaganda campaign could be developed. The opportunity was there for any Bonaparte with the ingenuity and courage to use it. It was seized by Louis Napoleon, who astounded his generation when he succeeded in re-creating a Bonapartist regime in France.

In his bid for power, he received no help from other members of the family. When he exhausted his inheritance from his mother, he was left to his own wiles to finance his cause. He was taken no more seriously by his family than by the public. For a time he had been engaged to Mathilde, Jerome's daughter, but she had broken off the match because he did not seem to have a very promising future. She came to rue this judgment when she realized that she could have been an empress. Nonetheless, she was an official hostess for Louis until he married, and during the Empire she and her brother always had an honored place at court. Their father, Jerome, the old ex-king of Westphalia, known after 1815 as the Count of Montfort, was also prominent after Louis came to power. In his most flagrant act of nepotism, Louis made the aged Bonaparte a marshal of France and Governor of the Invalides. Considering his debt to the Napoleonic legend, this was perhaps not too irrational an act. After

1848 there were few important living reminders of the First Empire, and every attempt was made to remind the public of past glories. That Jerome had never been personally popular made it seem inappropriate and something of a mistake, but Louis needed the support of the family and this gesture seemed little enough. Jerome and Prince Napoleon, however, proved difficult to placate.

Others in the family were no special asset, and Lucien's son, Prince Pierre, was a particular source of scandal. In 1870 this cousin of Napoleon III launched an editorial attack on critics of the Empire. He created further scandal when he murdered a young reporter serving as a second while negotiating a duel. Other relatives, though not such a problem, did expect money and favors. Like his uncle, the Emperor put up with them, simply because it was the easiest thing to do. Of all the family in his generation, it appears that Prince Napoleon really was the only other one with marked ability, and as time passed he became more cooperative. He finally became the Bonapartist pretender after the death of Louis' son, the Prince Imperial, in 1879. A source of political intrigue, the Third Republic exiled him in 1886 and he died in 1891, his heirs becoming successively the claimants to a Bonapartist crown.

The Intriguer and His Rise to Power

Louis Napoleon seemed born for intrigue; it was part of his nature. He was so much a conspirator and plotter that it is hard to give him adequate credit for his accomplishments that were aboveboard. He first attracted public attention in France through two coups attempting to overthrow Louis Philippe. These were amateurishly organized and failed completely. His twenty-two years of power were filled largely with scheming, and after his exile, the remaining three years of his life were spent planning a return. For a man who spent so much of his life plotting, it is remarkable that his most important acquisition of power came through an open and legal election in 1848.

Louis did not give the impression of being a vigorous attacker of the status quo. Many revolutionaries and intriguers have a streak of ruthlessness in their makeup, and in a crisis they reveal a core of cold, solid steel. However, Louis Napoleon showed himself to be humane and tender—indeed, deficient in exactly the qualities normally associated with an authoritarian regime. There was an undisciplined air about the man. He liked to speculate and to dream. Such men often fade after a season because they usually lack practical skill, the members of the Frankfort Assembly being a case in point. There were, in fact, many in France then who insisted that Louis Napoleon was like most of the impractical professorial men in that ill-fated group. They were mistaken, however, for Louis was one Forty-eighter still in power two decades later.

The Bonaparte family was, of course, Italian and always felt a special closeness to Italy. Here Napoleon had won some of his most striking victories and here most of his brothers and sisters spent their last years. The young Louis Napoleon was raised in exile and, from living in Augsburg and Arenenberg, learned to speak French with a German accent. Appropriately, his first appearance as a disturber of the status quo was in Italy in 1831. With his older brother, Napoleon Louis, he participated in the revolt in the Romagna, for a time actually controlling the town of Civita-Castellana. When the rebellion against Papal forces was put down by Austrian troops, Louis escaped, but his brother died, the victim of a measles epidemic. Although the revolt was short-lived, for the career of Louis Napoleon it had a lasting effect. He was afterwards identified with Italian aspirations for independence; he was suspected of membership in the Carbonari, and Italian revolutionaries continued to regard him as one of their number.

No other Bonaparte since 1815 had so daringly and openly challenged any regime. It was an important episode in Louis Napoleon's life and indeed a chapter in the history of Bonapartism, then only an embryonic movement in need of a new leader who would create a new following. One of the victims of the Italian exploit had been Andrea Orsini, a veteran of the Grand Army. Orsini was a tie to the past, and his son Felice later used an assassin's bomb to remind Louis of the task he had left unfinished in Italy.

In late October of 1836 Louis made his first bid for power in France. His appeal was direct and unequivocal. Speaking as a Bonaparte, he appeared before Napoleon's old regiment, the Fourth Artillery garrisoned at Strasbourg. He proposed a march on Paris and the downfall of Louis Philippe and was rewarded by cries of "Vive L'Empereur!" His attempt to gain control of the garrison was frustrated by quick action of the commander, and Louis was captured. Though he had earlier gained some of the officers' support, he concluded later that his mistake had merely been in neglecting to win over the one man who was responsible for his arrest. Heartened by the troops' response to his appeal, he told himself that had he been willing to order the commander killed, the coup would have succeeded. Bloodshed, however, was not part of his plan. He wanted to present France with a sort of replaying of Napoleon's return from Elba. Appearing at a frontier post, he would march on Paris, gaining support in each community en route. Thus arriving in Paris with a sizable army, he hoped to take over the government without violence and bloodshed, thus repeating the remarkable feat of his uncle. A simple appeal to Napoleonic memories would suffice. His attempt at Strasbourg had failed because of a tactical error in planning. He remained convinced that his basic plan was sound.

The government of Louis Philippe decided that it would be an error to publicize the young prince by a trial, so he was given money, dispatched to America and told never to return to France. He spent barely six months in the New World, mainly New York and Philadelphia, before he recrossed the Atlantic to renew contacts in London and in Switzerland. The Bonaparte family's most enthusiastic supporter and propagandist, J. G. Victor Fialin, later the Duc de Persigny, was waiting for him and ready for another adventuresome descent on France. Commonly regarded as more Bonapartist than any of the Bonapartes, Persigny had been at Strasbourg and was to spend the rest of his life working in the interests of Louis Napoleon. His unswerving loyalty and dedication, however, were almost continuously offset by impetuous blunders and tactless mistakes.

In 1840 another march on Paris was attempted. The mistake of Strasbourg was not repeated. General Magnan, commander of the northern military district, had been contacted and he agreed to support a march on Paris. This time the insurgents entered France from England. With a small group Louis landed at Boulogne, but neither soldiers nor townspeople responded to his appeals, so the party retreated. A number of Louis' party, including Persigny and the Prince, managed to get back to their boats; but in the turmoil, the boats capsized. A *Punch* cartoon showed the future emperor being fished out of the water on a boat hook.

Again his scheme had failed largely through an error in planning, but Louis may have correctly judged the mood of France. Louis

Philippe's regime was embarrassed by what Adolphe Thiers regarded as a cowardly role in the Eastern Crisis of 1840. Louis' *Napoleonic Ideas* had sold widely in France since its appearance the year before, and a resurgence of Napoleonic enthusiasm was sure to attend the return of Bonaparte's body from Saint Helena, the so-called Return of the Ashes.

Louis Philippe now decided that a formal trial was necessary to discredit the Prince once and for all. Louis Napoleon, however, took advantage of the occasion to make a broader appeal to France. Though his attempts to gain power had failed miserably, he had aroused some curiosity. Few in France had ever seen him or heard him speak. At his trial Louis denied that Louis Philippe's regime and its court (the Chamber of Peers) had any jurisdiction to try him for any offense against the French people, and he refused any consideration of mercy. He spoke both to and beyond the court and dramatically announced: "I stand before you the representative of a principle, a cause, a defeat. The principle is the sovereignty of the people; the cause is that of the Empire; the defeat is Waterloo."

However, there could be no doubt of his guilt, so he was sentenced to prison at Ham. As he left for prison, there was no question that despite the failure of his comic-opera coups and his subsequent condemnation, Louis had established himself as the Napoleonic pretender.

The incarceration at Ham proved to be a genteel version of prison life. Louis read widely and carried on a voluminous correspondence. He later referred to his six years' imprisonment as attending the "University of Ham." He played the role of lover, thanks to his jailer's tolerance, and wrote articles on a variety of subjects before time began to weigh heavily on his hands. In May, 1846, he put on the garb of a worker named Badinguet, balanced a board on his shoulder and walked out of the prison. Within a day he was in London. His father died in July, 1846, leaving Louis a modest inheritance which enabled him to resume a prominent place in English society.

In 1848 revolutionary mobs toppled Louis Philippe's regime with amazing ease. A shaky republican-socialist coalition then guided the nation while a grim struggle for power was developing. Persigny was in Paris publicizing the Prince and agitating for his cause. In April elections to the Assembly, three of Louis' cousins were elected: Prince Pierre, the son of Lucien; Prince Napoleon, the son of Jerome; and Lucien Murat, the son of Bonaparte's sister,

Caroline. In by-elections to the Assembly on June 4, Louis' name was entered for the first time, and he was elected in four departments. Many politicians were aghast. This Bonapartist pretender was technically an escaped criminal, and his election caused so much furor within the Assembly that despite his formal right to be seated, he remained in England and resigned the post ten days later. In late June the political struggle was played out in the streets of Paris. The army, commanded by General Cavaignac, engaged in a bloody slaughter of socialist-led mobs of urban proletariat. For the moment this brutal experience crushed the socialists and sobered the republicans. Efforts to frame a constitution were intensified.

Meanwhile, in supplementary assembly elections in September, Louis Napoleon was again elected. This time he returned from England and took his seat. His maiden speech misled many people. His Swiss-German accent sounded odd to Parisian ears; his mien suggested sluggishness; he lacked oratorical poise. The impression spread that he had been overrated because of his name and that a limited intelligence had been responsible for the failure of his two coup attempts.

As the presidential election drew near, publicity for Louis Napoleon reached fever heat. He emerged as the main opponent of General Cavaignac, who had "saved" the republic and expected his reward. Louis Napoleon's cause now attracted several opportunists like Adolphe Thiers who, lacking wide support themselves, expected to come to power under the mantle of the Bonaparte name. To the amazement of everyone, Louis Napoleon received more than 5,500,-000 votes while Cavaignac polled fewer than 1,500,000, with the republican poet-politician Alphonse Lamartine attracting barely 18,800. A man that very few Frenchmen knew had been elected to a four-year term as President of the Second Republic. Clearly he had won because of his name. The Napoleonic legend had paid off.

The new president was hardly in office when he began plans to convert the republic he was sworn to uphold into a Napoleonic empire. He carefully cultivated the idea that he was a protector and spokesman for the general public, opposing the hostile Assembly bent on diminishing popular sovereignty.

Another adherent to Bonapartism, General Emile Fleury, was now of particular importance. Regardless of who nominally held the office of war minister during the Republic, Fleury was the main presidential advisor on military matters. His immediate task was to make sure the army could be counted upon when the day came to move openly against the Assembly. Having campaigned in Algeria, Fleury was acquainted with many in the officer corps; now he saw to it that ambitious officers loyal to Bonapartism were transferred to key posts. The move of the notoriously opportunistic General Leroy de Saint-Arnaud from Algeria to Paris as minister of war in August of 1851 was a prelude to the coup and was recognized as such by Assembly members, who grumbled about the appointment but lacked the unity to do much else.

In addition to Persigny, Fleury and Saint-Arnaud, a key member of the plot to overthrow the Second Republic was Louis' half-brother, Morny. He proved to be an efficient organizer, lending an air of professionalism to the whole undertaking.

At this time supporters of Louis were deliberately publicizing the President as a champion of popular sovereignty and the Assembly as an enemy of the franchise. The constitution lacked a formula to resolve such a situation. It also prohibited the re-election of a president. Louis requested alteration of this provision so that he could succeed himself. The Assembly refused. This body contained only a minority in favor of maintaining the Republic, and many Orleanists (supporters of the dynasty of Louis Philippe) who were as much against the system as the Bonapartists. The issue really was over what sort of regime would take the Republic's place rather than the continuance of the Republic itself.

When the Assembly refused Louis' request, he resorted to force to resolve his and the government's dilemma. After tentative consideration of earlier dates, the coup finally was carried out on December 2, 1851, anniversary of both Napoleon's founding of the First Empire in 1804 and his greatest military triumph, the battle of Austerlitz in 1805. The evening of December 1 found Louis Napoleon and his fellow conspirators fulfilling routine social obligations and then meeting at the presidential palace where final plans were reviewed. Afterwards, while Louis slept, proclamations dissolving the Assembly and restoring popular sovereignty were secretly printed by Louis' fellow conspirators and quickly distributed so that people on their way to work the next morning saw them. Morny took over the ministry of the interior while the army controlled the city. A number of deputies to the Assembly were temporarily arrested to forestall a countercoup.

The general public, and especially the working class, accepted the change with a sense of humor. Republican agitators, however, began to organize resistance, and on December 4 and 5 a number of skirmishes occurred in Paris. Government troops killed more than 200 by "official" count (more than 400 probably), and Louis authorized widespread arrests and deportation of socialists and republicans. This effectively crushed opposition but left bad feeling. The dead were relatively few for a major change of government by force; still, enraged republicans for years referred to Louis as the Man of Blood and to his methods as illegal and murderous.

A plebiscite after the fact approved Louis' overthrow of the Assembly. Now, in Bonapartist terminology, the Republic entered a consular phase. The title of Prince-President became more widely used, and many of the trappings of the old empire reappeared. Louis, on a speaking tour of the provinces, openly speculated about what a move to empire would mean. While Europe's diplomats debated whether the appearance of a Bonaparte in France as an emperor—a clear violation of the Vienna settlement of 1815—would be an occasion for war, Louis sought to dispel their anxieties. He assured them that the empire would mean peace and that in those modern times it was no longer appropriate to fight over such things as boundaries or border provinces. Rather, he suggested, he wanted his victories to be in such fields as social improvements, swamp clearance and transportation. While Europe was still speculating, he made the final transition to empire on the anniversary of the coup. On December 2, 1852, he took the title of Napoleon III, Emperor of the French. He was to reign for nearly eighteen years.

The Military Expert

Any Bonaparte who would take advantage of the Napoleonic legend had to present himself as an expert on military affairs. Louis avidly studied the campaigns of Napoleon Bonaparte, reading everything available, particularly anything written by Napoleon himself.

His formal exposure to military life was limited. In 1829 Louis was enrolled in a Swiss artillery school, but he dropped out to participate in the abortive uprising in Italy in the spring of 1831. He then considered but declined an invitation to lead Polish insurgents. In 1834 he was commissioned as a captain of artillery in the Swiss army. This was a negligible military experience, since his duties were only seasonal and part-time, but the formal connection with Switzerland was most important. His commission had been granted in recognition of his *Military and Political Considerations on Switzerland* (1833). He followed this study with a *Manual of Artillery* (1834), which, to his delight, was officially adopted by the Swiss army and gave Louis proper credentials as a military authority.

During his imprisonment at Ham he read intensively over the whole range of military history, wrote many essays on technical aspects of warfare and began a major revision of his *Manual*. On leaving prison in 1846, he had a respectable store of military knowledge. Much of his writing was a blend of detail and propaganda, as illustrated in his later history of Julius Caesar. When he portrayed Caesar, the man he really had in mind was Napoleon Bonaparte. He stressed the importance of a key historical figure appearing at a crucial juncture in human history. Louis insisted that this work have a factual base, and his detailed questioning of experts led to fresh archaeological research that turned up new evidence on the Roman conquest and occupation of Gaul. In this, as in most of his work, he consciously tailored his message and language to an audience understood to include specialists, diplomats and literate peasants. He intended his serious and scholarly contributions to knowledge to serve also as deliberate propaganda.

This sort of writing by the Emperor appeared occasionally in the official government newspaper, *Le Moniteur Universel*. In the issue of April 11, 1855, Napoleon III discussed the first year of the Crimean War, in language described by Karl Marx as "the half-familiar, half-dignified style, characteristic of the man who writes at the same time for French peasants and for European cabinets." The article mixed fact and insinuation. A war which had never been really popular was being publicly criticized at home, and its continued cost in money and men needed justification. The Emperor declared that his generals had acted with courage and brilliance in circumstances of extreme difficulty. On the matter of invading the Crimea, he wrote that he would have landed elsewhere (Kaffa), but since the generals on the spot had decided differently, a chance to end the war quickly had been missed. He followed this implied criticism of his commanders with a militarily naive discussion that might sound reasonable to a layman. After this censure he defended his generals by explaining why Sebastopol was so difficult to capture. He declared that since Sebastopol was an unusual sort of fortress, many of the traditional procedures did not apply. This portion of his explanation could only have been for the French public and simply cannot be taken seriously. It was propaganda littered with technical terminology. His object was not to tell the truth but to defend his conduct of the war.

The Emperor's ideas as expressed in such propaganda should not be confused with his real knowledge of military affairs. His judgment as a military adviser can be seen from another look at the Crimean War. In this struggle Louis felt a strong urge to go to the front himself—to direct personally the allied armies—and it was only with reluctance that he allowed himself to be dissuaded. When Sebastopol did not readily fall and the war turned into a protracted siege, he began to send his generals all sorts of advice. He referred them to examples from Bonaparte's career as well as to some of his own compositions written at Ham. When these were not tried at once, Louis demanded explanations, and with the advent of the telegraph his generals suddenly found themselves in an exposed and weakened position. Counterarguments sounded like excuses for inaction; only General Pelissier had the nerve to ignore imperial dispatches.

How good was Louis' advice? Several of the allied generals in the Crimea tended to discount it completely, but this hardly did the Emperor justice. Louis Napoleon had worked out a fairly careful plan which he thought would bring the fall of Sebastopol. It involved splitting the allied force into three major units. One would man the trenches, another would march inland toward Baktschi-Serai and the third would land east of Balaclava at Aloushta and march inland toward Simpheropol. The Russian forces at Simpheropol would be forced into a battle to their disadvantage, and Sebastopol, at last cut off from its source of supplies, would fall. While this plan posed its own problems, it was more original and thoughtful than any proposed by a French or English general. In the absence of aggressive activity the Emperor became insistent that "his plan" be put into effect. The English generals refused to cooperate, and General Canrobert lacked the will to insist. In General Niel the Emperor had a representative on the spot, continually urging that his ideas be adopted. In the end the fortress fell after a sequence of events that amounted to a chance following of portions of the Emperor's plan. At the battle of the Tchernaya the Russians were defeated and Sebastopol was finally cut off from effective contact with Simpheropol. The Emperor's use of General Niel as a personal representative was particularly irksome to the officers with the day-to-day responsibility for operations. It fostered distrust between the generals and their sovereign and led the former to withhold information. Nonetheless, Napoleon III believed the idea was sound, and as late as the Mexican expedition still adhered to the practice. Then General Castelnau was his agent.

As a commander in the field the Emperor may best be judged by the campaign in Italy in 1859 and the victories of Magenta (June 4) and Solferino (June 24). Like so many attempts to evaluate Louis Napoleon, the results must remain inconclusive.

Magenta brought the Emperor face to face with the complexities of commanding an army in motion before an enemy. His troops were poorly provisioned and hardly prepared for the task that his diplomacy had made necessary. He was leading a Franco-Piedmontese force of about 150,000 men against an Austrian army of 110,000. At Magenta the Austrians made a stand and after eight hours were finally beaten by a combination of French infantry valor and the timely arrival of French reinforcements. The Emperor lacked a steady and accurate flow of information from his major units and at first thought that the engagement had been a defeat. He blamed Piedmont's King Victor Emmanuel for not having responded aggressively enough. He was aghast, as he surveyed the field of combat, at the large numbers of dead and dying. This aspect of war he had never encountered before, and the impact on him was profound.

At Magenta there was little indication that the Emperor had a clearer view of the situation than anyone else. His ideas and his grasp of things surely deserve no special credit. Solferino, however, was different, although the French were still woefully ill-prepared to fight a major opponent. The armies clashed, largely by accident, and this time the Austrians enjoyed a numerical advantage—190,000 men to 174,000. Several separate battles raged within eight miles of hilly terrain that made communications difficult. Napoleon III recognized that the struggle for Solferino in the center of the front was crucial and ordered an intensive effort accordingly. When the Austrians began to withdraw he sensed that they should be sharply pursued. His troops, however, were by then too fatigued for this, and a fierce thunderstorm helped end the fighting. Again the casualties impressed the Emperor, but this time there was also a resounding triumph that was uniquely his own. In his entire career this battle was Louis' only personal major military victory.

Louis Napoleon's remaining military involvement was in the Franco-Prussian War in 1870. Though he was by then seriously ill, the Emperor defied the advice of his doctors, who counseled against his going to the front. His name was Napoleon, and Eugénie was continuously reminding him that he had an obligation to direct the armies personally. With his son, the Prince Imperial, Napoleon arrived at Metz on July 28 to command an invasion of Germany. He expected to move quickly into Baden, detaching some of the south German states. In the meantime reserves would be gathering in France. Diplomatically, the result would be to entice Austria and Italy to enter the war on the side of France. Gross logistical errors forced cancellation of this plan. An attack on Saarbrücken (which turned out to be successful) was approved by the Emperor, more for its propaganda value than anything else, but major offensive action was out of the question. In the next weeks the Emperor was continuously in pain; the crucial military judgments were made by Marshal Bazaine, and the Emperor was reduced to a mere spectator.

As in other campaigns of the Second Empire, when it came to specific suggestions Napoleon's ideas were as sound as those of his generals. In 1870 his suggestions for coordinating troop movements and keeping the road to Paris blocked to the enemy revealed his good common sense. However, logistical failures coupled with Bazaine's mistakes doomed the Empire.

As the head of his government for over two decades, Louis Napoleon must shoulder much of the blame for the shortages and obsolescence that characterized French arms in many of their engagements. Indeed, the failure to keep the army modernized was perhaps his major blunder. It is a shocking indictment that in 1870 the French, who were so technologically up to date in the Crimean War, could be defeated by an army distinguished mainly by its modernization and leadership. For this Napoleon III was largely responsible. His army was rarely well prepared for any of its later campaigns. The Emperor was a clever propagandist capable of some insights in military affairs, but he was a mediocre administrator. It is amazing that such a regime which capitalized on militarism and engaged in successive wars lasted as long as it did.

The Socialist Writer

A common witticism about the Second Empire portrayed the

Emperor referring to Eugénie as a legitimist, Morny an Orleanist, Prince Napoleon a republican, and himself a socialist. The only Bonapartist was Persigny, who was crazy. The reference to himself as a socialist is particularly intriguing; but, like many labels one might think of for Louis Napoleon, it fits somewhat uncomfortably.

Louis could readily pass as another ideologue in an age overrich in that commodity. His political ambitions were so great that there can be no question that most of what he wrote for publication was designed to contribute to his career.

He did, however, have a genuine feeling for people and a particular interest in social and economic problems. During his confinement at Ham he studied extensively and, as well as writing military history, contributed many newspaper articles commenting on a wide range of current events. The sugar beet industry in France especially attracted his attention. Napoleon Bonaparte had fostered this industry after Britain's naval response to his Continental System interrupted the easy flow of trade between France and the West Indies. Subsequently, home industry came to rival the colonial producers, and debate raged in France over whether or not the government should still be giving it subsidies and protection. Louis strongly supported the industry in France. While this reflected his belief in an active government role in economic affairs, at the same time appealing to businessmen interested in protectionism, his later support for free trade probably is a truer gauge of his beliefs, since by then he was in power and obviously not catering for business support. It should be noted that Morny, his half-brother, was deeply involved financially in the sugar beet industry. Thus, Louis may not have been giving merely an intellectual opinion when he supported its protection.

His most important writing on the role of government in promoting economic change was his *L'Extinction du Pauperisme*, a short pamphlet written at Ham in 1844. This established him as a champion of the workers. Surprisingly free of references to Napoleon Bonaparte, the narrative discussed the unemployment caused mainly by the exodus from the countryside to the cities. His solution was for the government to relocate the workers on vast tracts still untilled. Here they would live in barracks and have a simple, military-like organization. The governors and other officials were to be elected, and he emphasized that these were *not* military colonies. They would be agricultural colonies, planned at first for twenty years. Napoleon Bonaparte had had ideas for retiring soldiers on unoccupied land, and Louis, in effect, was adapting this plan to the special conditions of the later, more industrial society.

In this pamphlet he included a considerable amount of statistical information which, he maintained, demonstrated that the colonies would readily produce profits, to the benefit of the whole society. They would, in fact, be so successful that he foresaw "branches in Algiers, and even in America; it may in time spread over the whole world!" His statistics lent an air of scientific authority to the scheme, and he explicitly stated that modifications should be made "in every particular where the experience of men versed in these complicated matters can furnish it with useful data and new lights."

Regardless of its practicality, Louis' plan was thoroughly humanitarian. He wanted to eliminate "the sources of ignorance, vice and misery." He would make the laborers proprietors; from the enjoyment of property rights they would acquire expectations, they would become educated, and France would prosper.

Almost parenthetically in his analysis, he mentioned a number of other interesting ideas. He noted, for example, that "the quantity of merchandise which a country exports is always in direct ratio with the number of *bullets* which it may fire at its enemies, when its honor and dignity command it to do so."

A program to eliminate pauperism, and perhaps poverty, obviously had enormous political potential. Louis posited a government much concerned with social problems, actively using its power for human betterment, a foreshadowing of Second Empire programs as well as a variety of state socialism. It is ironic that these ideas about the establishment of agricultural colonies, formulated when Louis was a young man, were never implemented when he became Emperor.

Louis' sympathy for the unemployed poor, expressed in this work, evoked the feeling for mankind found in the writing of the utopian socialists, especially Henri de Saint-Simon, Charles Fourier and Louis Blanc. With Fourier and Blanc, Louis Napoleon was also suggesting the relocation of workers in new communities, though Fourier put far more emphasis on the agrarian aspects of the new society. For Louis the agrarian colonies were to supplement a developing urbanism which happened to have a surplus of labor. He did not glorify rural life as such. His pamphlet attracted praise from many intellectuals, and Louis Blanc took the trouble to visit him in prison for firsthand discussions.

The greatest French critic of the developing capitalistic system was Joseph Proudhon, who was also attracted briefly to Louis Napoleon. Proudhon, however, was far too thoroughgoing for most other reformers, Louis included. He wanted a complete moral revolution which would come through economic freedom and justice. Ultimately government and the state would disappear—hardly an idea the Bonapartist pretender could find congenial. Implicit in his philosophy was a threat not only to the future authority of Napoleon III but to all other governments in Europe as well.

One of the themes in Louis Napoleon's earlier *Napoleonic Ideas* was that Napoleon I had achieved great works in the area of social reform. While other theorizers looked ahead to some experimental recasting of governmental functions, Louis Napoleon tied most of his pleas for reform to the idea of a restored empire following a successful pattern already tried by his uncle. This was still his idea on October 9, 1852, at Bordeaux when he spoke of the character of any new Bonapartist empire in France. He spoke for peace, for conciliation and for the spread of Christ's gospel. And he spoke of vast programs of improved communications and productivity. All of these were to be achieved "like the Emperor" in an imperial structure assuring the solid conquest of social problems.

His Ladies and His Court

Louis Napoleon made a name for himself as conspirator, prisoner, president and emperor. He also played the part of an aging Don Juan. This aspect of his character made him appear disreputable to many and gave his political opponents a powerful propaganda issue, which was especially damning when accompanied with the omnipresent references to the illegitimacy of Morny, his minister of the interior and half-brother, and to rumors questioning his own paternity. Louis, a conspirator against established governments, was also no respecter of marriage vows or traditional moral standards. The best that could be said for his amorous ventures was that he seemed to confine himself to one affair at a time.

The first episode of note took place during his imprisonment at Ham. In an extended affair with a local girl, Alexandrine Vergeot, he fathered two sons, Eugene and Ernest, born in 1843 and 1845 respectively. Though he kept track of his sons and made sure that they both became counts with good positions, his interest in their mother appears to have ceased when he left Ham.

Leaving the arms of Alexandrine Vergeot, he shortly found similar solace and affection from Elizabeth Ann Haryett, generally known as Lady Howard. From mid-1846 to mid-1848 they lived together as husband and wife but for the formality of a wedding ceremony. In 1846 she was twenty-three years old and strikingly beautiful. An attempt at a theatrical career had been only moderately successful, but two experiences as a mistress had left her with a considerable fortune and one son, Martin. Louis seems to have been genuinely happy while living with Lady Howard, and he entrusted to her the upbringing of his two sons. The three children were raised as brothers, and gossips attributed all three to the illicit relations of Louis Napoleon and Lady Howard. Though they lived and loved together, no child was born from their affection.

Large sums for the campaign to propel Louis to the presidency in 1848 and also to finance the founding of the Empire came from Miss Howard. Through most of his presidency she was still his mistress, frequently appearing with him in public. The creation of the Empire, however, called for a wife of genuine nobility, and gradually the two parted. While Louis had many more affairs, Lady Howard, calling herself the Comtesse de Beauregard, retired to an estate, doting on her memories and the tragedy of how a great love had been cut short because of political success.

Lady Howard's problem was that as Louis became successful, scheming and beautiful women threw themselves at his feet. Among the women Louis knew, the cleverest was Eugénie, the woman he married. He was dazzled by her beauty, but she adamantly refused his advances unless he would go to the altar. Eugénie was a minor member of the Spanish nobility. Known as Mlle. de Montijo, the Countess de Teba, she was presented by her mother as a devoutly religious virgin, a precious commodity well worth marrying. She was, however, impoverished and would bring no dowry. Many of Louis' associates advised that she would add little strength to an imperial crown; but love triumphed over reason, and he married her. There was genuine affection between them for only a very short time. No woman who found intimate relations to be merely disgusting, as Eugénie did, could hope to hold Louis' loyalty. Though she felt jealous, her vanity wounded, still she preferred to ignore much of his philandering rather than provide the gratification he seemed to need. After miscarriages endangering her life, she gave birth to an heir, the Prince Imperial, on March 16, 1856. Frightened by her brush with death, she regarded her obligations fulfilled now that a son was born and emphatically rejected the Emperor as a bed companion.

A succession of other affairs followed, which gossip avidly reported. The Emperor found conquests easier and easier, and his reputation as a disreputable rake grew. Diplomats tried to take advantage of his weakness. Caustic observers noted that illegitimacy seemed to be the rule. Morny openly flaunted his origins, and on occasion directing the French foreign ministry was Count Alexandre Walewski, the illegitimate son of a double adultery by Napoleon I and the Polish Countess Walewska. That Napoleon III became a lover of the Florentine Marie de Ricci, Walewski's second wife, seemed scandalous to the critics, but appropriate to their view of the Empire's immoral and degenerate character. Another Italian beauty, the Countess de Castiglione, was related to Cavour, who instructed her to win the Emperor's favor and then convince him of the need to help Italy. Though it is doubtful Louis paid much attention to her comments about Italy, he enjoyed her sensuous attractions to the full.

In later years, troubled by gallstones, the Emperor's appetite for women seemed not to diminish, though his strength was waning swiftly. However, after Lady Howard and his initial infatuation with Eugénie, Louis seemed never to have enjoyed real happiness with any woman. In January of 1865, a particularly sordid two-year affair came to an end—his liaison with Marguerite Bellanger. A tomboyish woman with a wide reputation for profligate vulgarity, she attracted Louis with her unsophisticated and unpolished manners. On one occasion, wracked with pain and weakened from his life of dissolution, Louis fainted at her house. Eugénie herself went to the woman, bluntly accused her of "killing the Emperor," and vainly offered her money to cast Napoleon aside. In this amazing confrontation, the conversation began with harsh and biting accusations but ended cordially, as the two found to their surprise that they sympathized with each other's position.

Though the Empress Eugénie failed her husband as a lover, she succeeded brilliantly as a leader in high society. Following her example the Second Empire became an exciting period in fashions and style. Most people accepted Eugénie as society's First Lady, but there were some exceptions and these annoyed her. Many members of the old nobility shunned the court, but it was even more irritating that within the Bonaparte family she was tolerated rather than accepted. At times Prince Napoleon was openly insulting. Louis' cousin Mathilde was not rude, but she viewed the Empress with a suppressed jealousy because she could never forget that she herself could have been the wife of the Emperor. Her disgust at Louis' indiscriminate pursuit of women made her sympathize with his wife, but she adamantly refused the Empress' efforts to become friends.

Eugénie presided over the most extravagant court in France since that of Louis XVI. She was the beautiful center of formal gatherings where gorgeous gowns and bemedaled uniforms were omnipresent. There were always a number of prominent foreigners at court, giving it a distinctively European flavor. This was due both to the new prestige of France after 1856 and to the acquaintances made by the Bonapartes in their years of exile.

Several diplomatic missions in Paris were headed by men whose wives were particularly attractive. Especially important was Princess Pauline Metternich, wife of the Austrian ambassador, who became in the 1860's nearly as prominent in the social whirl as the Empress. Intensely interested in women's fashion, she helped to establish Parisian styles.

The court moved with the seasons. Winters were spent at the Tuileries, summers at Saint-Cloud and Fontainebleau, while November was usually given over to hunting parties at Compiègne. In the entire year only one month was free of elaborate entertainment. Each September the Emperor and Empress went to Biarritz near the Spanish border to relax and to forget the burdens they carried the rest of the year.

Court life, despite its lavishness, was described as superficial by many contemporaries. The inevitable and obligatory formality of any official imperial gathering was partly responsible for this. Royalty from old houses mingled with *parvenus*, the most prominent *parvenu* being the Emperor himself, and helped create a situation where all were self-conscious. Another factor was the background and taste of the Emperor. Many of his personal inclinations and habits can best be described as bourgeois. This was very clear at Biarritz where Louis and Eugénie lived in an unsophisticated fashion. At formal dinners in the Tuileries and elsewhere it was evident in the menus that were served. Neither of the imperial couple cared much for food, and members of the older aristocracy as well as other critics of the regime made caustic comments about second-rate, bourgeois fare.

Entertainment at court also was rather trivial, featuring spelling-bees, charades and skits. Masked balls were exceptionally popular, suiting well the needs of a court filled with people whose stock-in-trade was deception and intrigue. Open opportunities for flirtations seemed to strike everyone's fancy, with the Emperor an eager participant.

Pleasure-seeking seemed a worthwhile objective to the court. Many values of the bourgeoisie were then being solidly established in society, and the Second Empire lent a strong impetus to this development, which had really started in 1830, when Louis Philippe, the businessman's champion, came to power. Paris, in 1870, was a city where theatrical productions designed only to entertain and amuse were in vogue. Theater was no longer aimed solely at the aristocracy; Paris developed a reputation as a city of lower-class drama and cheap pleasures. There was still intellectual vigor in France, but not particularly in its imperial court. Horse racing and gambling were popular past-times for those who could afford it and the Jockey Club was an especially prestigious organization.

Salons were in fashion but most were given over to banal conversation and gossip. The most intellectually stimulating salon was presided over by Princess Mathilde. Her house was a meeting place for such prominent intellectuals as Ernest Renan, Hippolyte Taine and Louis Pasteur, as well as politicians like Emile Ollivier and writers of the stature of Gustave Flaubert. There, ideas were introduced, criticized and debated—but the ground rules demanded that exchanges were not to be heated, calm good manners were to prevail and nobody was to criticize Napoleon I. There were many other salons but none as attractive to persons of intellectual stature. Indeed, the others ranged down to the level of simple café society. None of the gatherings presided over by the Emperor and Empress could be remotely referred to as a salon, since there was too much emphasis on either stilted formalism or shallow entertainment.

Chapter 3

Imperial Foreign and
Domestic Problems

The Authoritarian Empire

Louis Napoleon's complete dismantling of the republican government had taken only one year. France was again an empire, ruled
once more by a Napoleon. A December, 1851, plebiscite had overwhelmingly approved the coup d'état, and another in November,
1852, sanctioned the final establishment of an imperial constitution.

The new system essentially unified authority in the nation. The
error of 1848 had been an excessive enthusiasm for Montesquieu's
famous principle of separation of powers. After the coup Louis
moved to devise a basic document that specifically repudiated this
doctrine. What emerged was a Bonapartist authoritarianism ending
the Second Republic. While Louis Napoleon was severely criticized
in some quarters for his callous betrayal of the constitution he had
sworn to uphold, the alternative would probably have been some
sort of Orleanist restoration. Survival of a republic was highly unlikely. Critics, noting the bloodshed and deportations that followed
the shift to empire should also have recalled that in July of 1851
Louis had tried to have his term of office legally prolonged. Alexis
de Tocqueville supported that idea, along with a majority of the
Assembly, but such a constitutional change required three-quarters

of the Assembly votes. When the balloting on July 19 demonstrated only a simple majority, force became the most likely alternative. Whether Louis might have won in another vote later in the year is problematical. He made no further legal effort to win over the Assembly, but accepted the idea of force. The illegality and bloodshed associated with his coup of December were to be continually recalled by political opponents, and in the sixties proved a heavy propaganda liability.

The legislative processes of the Second Empire, described in the Constitution of 1852, copied closely those of the First Empire. A Senate of dignitaries (constitutionally set at between 80 and 150, 72 the first year), selected for life by Louis Napoleon, was to study the validity of legislative bills and to act as interpreters of the constitution. Bills were to be drawn up, presented and defended by a Council of State, a body of 40 to 50 appointees serving at the pleasure of Louis Napoleon. Measures were debated and voted upon by a popular house called the Legislative Body, whose 260 members served six-year terms and met in annual three-month sessions. Louis Napoleon had the right to select the president and vice-president of this chamber from among its membership. The ministers heading the major bureaucratic organs of government could not be members of the Legislative Body (that is, drawn from the popularly elected body), but served in the Council of State and usually the Senate.

Napoleon III could count on complete control everywhere except in the Legislative Body. Even here he could be assured of direct parliamentary control through his right to select the president, and during much of his reign his influence extended through the whole Body. Elections to this lower house were accompanied by subtle government pressures and "surveillance." It was a great asset in most localities to be the government candidate. Pro-Bonapartist candidates were elected in large numbers, and there was little danger of the popular house being antagonistic to Napoleon during most of the Empire. Also, the government freely gerrymandered the districts to enhance the chances of its own candidates. A sign of enlightenment or perhaps maturity was the Emperor's willingness to work through existing elites. Thus in many areas one did not need to be a Bonapartist to be an official candidate, and it was possible for the regime to attract the nominal support of many Orleanists and other local men of substance and prestige. They discovered that they could serve Napoleon III with little difficulty since his system, despite its symbols and terminology of the First Empire, varied only moderately from that of Louis Philippe's July Monarchy. The Emperor proved willing to go more than halfway to satisfy the interests of other parties, though in return he required from all public officials an oath of obedience to the constitution and to himself. Overlooking his own record as a violator of the constitution at the time of the coup, he nonetheless believed that most people took oaths seriously, and so it was an essential part of his imperial structure. While repugnance at the oath led a few men to carry retirement from public life, large numbers were able to overcome their scruples in order to be a part of the system, enjoying the prestige and advantages that favor in Paris could bring.

One of the Second Empire's most embarrassing problems in foreign affairs stemmed from a bold move by Louis Napoleon in 1849. As President of the Second Republic he sent an expedition to Rome to defend Pius IX, thereby crushing a newly formed republic. This gesture, apparently expected to win broad Catholic support in France, alienated Italian republicans, whom Louis tried to appease by pressuring the Pope to carry through reforms. Pius IX was only moderately cooperative, and French troops remained in Rome almost continuously until 1870. An alternative to this French initiative in 1849 would have been Austrian intervention, and Louis argued that his action was to prevent a further increase of Austrian strength in Italy.

The Empire was born under another cloud in foreign affairs. In the months after the coup d'état statesmen discussed the situation in France in terms of the treaties of 1815, which explicitly forbade the restoration of a Bonapartist Empire in France. Louis Napoleon had been a welcome relief after the disorders and socialistic threats of 1848. He appeared dedicated to public order and strong enough to assure it—but to restore the Empire was something else again. Since most diplomats assumed that after the coup he would successfully take complete control, the debate came to settle on the pros and cons of which numeral he might take. To call himself Napoleon III seemed to imply both dynastic succession and a blunt challenge to the treaties signed at Vienna. His assumption of this title created mild consternation in other courts, but only Nicholas of Russia declared himself ready to march in defense of the sanctity of treaties and the settlement of 1815. However, he would not march alone, and so the establishment of a new empire and a new Napoleon went essentially unchallenged. Textbooks often note that in a childish gesture the Tsar had his ambassador's credentials indicate Louis Napoleon as a "friend" rather than a "brother," and that Napoleon, petulant over the slight, turned to an anti-Russian foreign policy. To see the incident this way is to overlook the fact that Nicholas had used this format in 1830 to express his disapproval of Louis Philippe's succession to Charles X. If Louis was annoyed, he was also relieved that Russian hostility took no more active a form.

In 1850 the aged Eastern Question entered a new phase as Louis Napoleon instructed his ambassador in Constantinople, General Aupick, to insist that France was the legal protector of Catholic pilgrims en route from western Europe to such holy places as Jerusalem and Bethlehem. This had been affirmed in numerous treaties with the Ottoman Empire, most recently in 1740. Resident in the Holy Land were several Roman Catholic (or Latin) orders which were to carry out certain stipulated duties of upkeep and repair of the shrines that, in the Sultan's view, then entitled the Catholics of Europe to the privilege of worshiping there. Since 1758, however, the Latins had neglected their responsibilities; many of their functions were taken over by Greek Orthodox Christians, who were given firmans or grants of authority by the Sultan as compensation for their efforts. In the early nineteenth century a series of disputes arose out of the conflict between the terms of the French treaty of 1740 and later firmans which frequently gave the same rights and privileges to the Orthodox Church. These disputes revolved about such points as which group should worship earliest in the day in a particular shrine or which should hold its keys. It was not a matter of possession but one of priority. Aupick and his successor, the Marquis de LaValette, were effective spokesmen for France; and the Sultan, characteristically yielding before threats, awarded the keys to the French but told the Greeks no change in practice would be made, a compromise that pleased none of the disputants.

So long as sponsorship of the Catholic position in the dispute over holy places could be easily accomplished, Louis readily gave it his support. By mid-1853, however, the complex issues centering at Constantinople had become so entangled that war with Russia loomed as a distinct possibility. This was more than Napoleon remotely had envisaged, and he became anxious. Louis would have welcomed any solution short of war, so his selection of the bellicose General Baraguay d'Hilliers as a new ambassador "to preach peace" was a strange choice. Though he repeatedly expressed his anxiety to Lord Cowley, the British ambassador in Paris, Napoleon had taken no steps to increase the size of the French army as late as November, 1853.

Many historians have argued that the French Emperor was chiefly responsible for the Crimean War, but it is now clear that Napoleon III was only one of many whose actions led to hostilities no nation or individual really wanted.

The Russian Tsar saw himself as the defender of the Orthodox Church and erroneously believed that the treaty of Kuchuk Kainardji (1774) gave him an explicit obligation to protect Orthodox Christians residing in the Ottoman Empire. He was a dedicated supporter of stability and order and the principles of the Congress of Vienna. An arch-conservative, he was positive that liberal movements were dangerous and had a phobia about the lurking presence of what he called The Revolution. He interpreted the French demands in Constantinople as The Revolution at work. Nicholas regarded the Ottoman Empire as a decaying institution and in 1844 had frankly discussed its dissolution with British leaders. Great Britain had cooperated with Russia in detaching Greece from Ottoman sovereignty and also was engaged in serious economic competition with Russia for the markets and produce of the Ottoman Empire. Russia had had influence in Constantinople for decades. In 1849 she had played a crucial role in crushing liberal movements and restoring order in central Europe. Had Nicholas desired to, in 1849 and 1850 he could have taken, without any opposition, virtually any part of the Ottoman Empire. To Nicholas, the Ottoman decision to award the keys to the French had favored the Latin Christians, and was a change of the status quo and a violation of the principles of 1815. The fact that Louis Napoleon was, in effect, a child of revolution did not help matters.

The Russian leader now decided that a forceful demonstration was needed to make the Turks change their mind on the awarding of the keys. At the end of February, 1853, his special emissary, Prince Menschikoff, arrived in Constantinople and with studied insolence and arrogance presented Russia's position. Having no idea what to do, the Sultan at first complied with many of Russia's demands. Meanwhile, French and British attachés sent their home governments reports that the situation was crucial and called for naval support for the Sultan. Napoleon sent the French fleet to Besika Bay outside the Dardanelles, while the British instructed their Mediterranean fleet to join the French, and their ambassador to Constantinople, Stratford de Redcliffe, hastily returned to his post from a vacation at home.

After this, Napoleon III's role in the diplomacy leading to the war was modest, as initiatives were seized by Stratford de Redcliffe. Menschikoff's demands were now refused by the Sultan who, with Stratford behind him, gave an uncharacteristic show of backbone. On May 21 Menschikoff left Constantinople, and the entire Russian legation followed. He expected that upon reflection the Turks would change their mind, but they did not. When no further word came, the Tsar ordered troops into the principalities of Moldavia and Wallachia to give the Russians weight in further negotiations. Nicholas explained that his action was not aggrandizement, but had merely been taken to balance the appearance of the allied warships in the East. The British and French responded by sending their fleets into the Black Sea in violation of the Straits Convention of 1841.

All Europe was now aware of the dangerous situation that had developed. The Austrians called a conference which feverishly arranged a settlement that would save everybody's face. This desperate attempt failed when a compromise, agreed to by all other parties, was refused by the Turks (at the suggestion of Stratford de Redcliffe). Napoleon was aghast; the Tsar was furious and unprepared for further negotiation and compromise. The Turks declared war and the chances of maintaining peace became remote. Tempers rose on all sides when the Turkish fleet was destroyed at Sinope on November 30, 1853, by the Russians.

As 1854 opened, Russia and Turkey were at war and the whirlpool threatened to involve the rest of Europe. The once-hopeful negotiations sponsored by Austria still dragged on; but after Sinope, the prospects were dim for a settlement without further use of armed force.

On March 12, 1854, a treaty of alliance was concluded at Constantinople between representatives of France, Great Britain and Turkey. These powers pledged to guarantee Ottoman integrity and independence. The Sultan invited France and Britain "to aid in repelling the aggression of His Majesty the Emperor of all the Russians . . . [and] to maintain the balance of power among the states of Europe." When Russia failed to answer an Anglo-French ultimatum to evacuate Moldavia and Wallachia, France entered the war against Russia on March 27, 1854. She joined Great Britain in a military alliance on April 10, ostensibly for the defense of Turkey. This was the first time in centuries that the British and French were allies rather than enemies in a major military contest; and that it occurred while France was under a Napoleon made it the more remarkable.

Most of the leaders of the French army had served with Fleury years before in Algeria and, when he called them to Paris, had proven their loyalty to Louis Napoleon at the time of the coup. As a group these new "chiefs of the Bonapartist army," as Fleury called them, were particularly ambitious. They were anxious to wipe away what they regarded as the stain of Waterloo. In 1847 there had been a number of Orleanist supporters as well as republicans in the upper ranks of the army. By 1852 many of these had gone into exile—the most distinguished being generals Changarnier, Cavaignac and Lamoricière. Of known republicans remaining in the army the most prominent was Bosquet, whom Fleury regarded as no danger to Napoleon III since he aspired for personal glory more than for republicanism—an observation that proved to be true.

Fleury's most important recruit from the Algerian campaigns was the adventurous and colorful Leroy de Saint-Arnaud, the minister of war who had directed the coup d'état. To Saint-Arnaud, now a marshal of France and deathly ill from angina and intestinal cancer, went the command of the Expedition to the East. He insisted on this last chance for personal glory and Napoleon had not the heart to refuse. Doctors expected him to live barely four months, possibly dying en route to Constantinople. As it turned out, he survived long enough to win a victory over the Russians.

The early months of the expedition were fraught with logistic confusion and a lack of agreement with the English regarding objectives. The "self-made, experienced African" generals of France seemed a low breed to the English officers, who were "gentlemen." The British commander, Lord Raglan, who had lost an arm at Waterloo, annoyed his allies by frequently praising Wellington and absentmindedly referring to the enemy as "the French."

The allied armies concentrated first at Varna, but Russian inactivity in this area plus a serious cholera outbreak led the generals finally to a decision to strike directly at Russia by landing in the Crimea. A brisk landing with a battle to settle the fate of Sebastopol was all they envisioned. They never considered that the battle might be lost, or that, as it proved, they might win the battle (Alma) without achieving the immediate fall of Sebastopol.

At the battle of Alma, Saint-Arnaud won the finest victory of his career. He had planned the battle and, despite English lagging, it had been fought as he anticipated. The engagement was of special interest because it showed the caliber of French leadership and troops in major combat, exposed for all Europe to see. Their Algerian experience was evident in the use of bayonets and the attack in broken lines. Also, French officers personally led their men as they moved at the enemy, an awesome force pouring heavy artillery fire into their midst. Among these officers was Prince Napoleon, who had been given a general's rank and commanded a division.

The battle had been fiercely contested, and rather than risk another such engagement, the allied commanders decided to march around Sebastopol and attack from the south where defenses were thought to be slight. By the time the armies were in place south of the city and had built up a massive supply of artillery ammunition, the defenders of the city had hastily erected new defenses which proved to be too strong for the allied forces, dooming them to the rigors of a winter in the Crimea. Saint-Arnaud had departed after his victory (dying en route home) and left General Canrobert in charge of the French forces.

When the full force of winter fell on the allied armies, the siege was as much against mud and nature as the Russians. Difficult as life was for the French, conditions were immeasurably worse for the English. Shortages of all sorts plagued both armies, but the French were better prepared for life in the field than their allies were. Before the winter settled in and made major military operations nearly impossible, there were two noteworthy engagements. On October 25, during the battle of Balaclava, the heralded "Charge of the Light Brigade" occurred, an episode of incredible folly and heroism which nullified advantages the English had gained earlier that day. On November 5 a major Russian attack on the allied position was repulsed, demonstrating that while the allies could not take Sebastopol, neither could they be driven away. This battle of Inkerman was a bloody allied victory. Then on November 14 a major hurricane turned the whole area into a muddy morass, sending several shiploads of supplies to the bottom of the Black Sea and immobilizing French, English and Russians alike.

In midwinter Sardinia joined the alliance against the Russians, ostensibly as an equal partner but actually in a mercenary role in pay of the English. They were well equipped, but their numbers were modest and they participated only briefly in one major engagement.

During winter and into the spring Canrobert's relations with Lord Raglan steadily worsened. Napoleon was annoyed that more was not being done at the front and replaced Canrobert with Pelissier, a gruff and surly veteran of Algerian campaigning.

The new commander's appointment coincided with a marked improvement in the weather in the Crimea and the allied armies assumed a more offensive posture. Pelissier deliberately disregarded "advice" which he received from Paris about how to conduct the siege, and only narrowly averted being relieved. Though he openly rejected the Emperor's ideas, his activities during the summer constituted a partial *de facto* acceptance of their validity. After unsuccessful allied assaults on Sebastopol in June, a Russian force attempting to relieve the city was beaten at Tchernaya, making Sebastopol's survival far more unlikely. Since the Russians were defeated on the approaches to the city, as Napoleon had urged, the siege could be intensified. On September 8, 1855, Sebastopol was taken in a massive assault.

After Sebastopol's fall, desultory expeditions went out to other points along the Black Sea coast. Nicholas had died and the new Tsar, Alexander II, was anxious for peace. Diplomats were now able to arrange an armistice, and a peace conference, the Congress of Paris, met in the spring of 1856.

At this Congress Napoleon III assumed the role of arbiter of Europe. He had reached the pinnacle of his career. In his person France spoke with more international authority than she had since Napoleon I. Russia, the real power in the coalition enforcing the Vienna settlement, had been humbled militarily and deserted diplomatically by both Austria and Prussia. England had even assisted in the Russian defeat. In terms of prestige, the French triumph was complete.

The war had likewise been a triumph for the French army.

French arms were crucial in every allied victory, and it was in the French sector during the final attack that the major breakthrough occurred leading to the fall of Sebastopol. Through most of the war, in terms of logistics, ordnance and ordinary know-how, the French army had been vastly superior to the English. The enthusiasm of victory, however, obscured an important change that had taken place. French medical services in the early phases of the war were outstanding. While wretched conditions prevailed in the English army, wounded Frenchmen received prompt and careful attention. However, as the war progressed and the English were belatedly improving, the French facilities gradually disintegrated until at the end of the war men were dying at an appalling rate from cholera and infectious disease. The tragedy of the army during the Second Empire is that immediately after the Crimean War there was no attempt to correct deficiencies the war had revealed. An army with a remarkable adaptive capacity and the ability to implement technical innovations was allowed to fall behind the times—ultimately to be overwhelmed by an army distinguished mainly by being technologically up-to-date.

In 1856, however, the mood was one of triumph. The Emperor gave marshals' batons to generals Bosquet and Canrobert. He also gave one to General Randon, who as minister of war in 1851 had helped in early preparations for the coup. Now as governor general of Algeria, his promotion signaled the end of the strictly military phases of the conquest. All three of these were ironic appointments. Bosquet had believed that his republican criticism of the coup would prevent the Emperor from ever allowing his elevation to the marshalate; Canrobert had never won a victory in the field; and Randon as a young officer had ordered troops to fire on Napoleon I during the latter's return from Elba.

The Congress of Paris was a public acknowledgment of Napoleon III's ascendancy. The English were present reluctantly; they had not looked good in the final assault on Sebastopol and resented French prominence in the diplomacy leading to the Congress. At the same time a Franco-Russian entente appeared to be developing which heightened English apprehensions regarding their ally.

Decisions at the Congress on the status of the principalities of Moldavia and Wallachia proved impractical, and activists there presented a tired Europe with the *fait accompli* of Rumanian independence. Though Napoleon favored independence for national groups, he was unprepared for the speed and tactics with which the new nation was created. The Rumanians invoked his name as one of their supporters and, to his embarrassment, Napoleon found that he had little choice but to sanction events already under way. The "Arbiter" had in effect been exploited by a remote situation in which he really had no control—a pattern destined to be often repeated.

The Growing Opposition

At the Congress of Paris, Cavour's emphatic indictment of Austrian rule in Italy served as a reminder that western Europe still had a major, unresolved problem. Napoleon listened with obvious interest but took no immediate action. He was at the apex of his career and appeared satisfied. At this point, however, his heritage as a Bonaparte would not allow him to disregard Italy and her problems. He had for years vaguely promised that one day he would "do something for Italy." His past Carbonari associations seemed to indicate a republican orientation, but in 1849 he had crushed the Roman republic and defended the Papacy. His justification that otherwise Austria would have filled this role and become even stronger in Italy was only partially convincing to Italian zealots. He had put off their pleas for aid against Austria, alleging that first he had to become master in France. After his coup another year passed in preparation for the proclamation of empire. By then the Eastern Question was alarming, and he was necessarily distracted from Italy by the Crimean War.

After Cavour's statements at the Congress reminding the Emperor that Italy's grievances must now be considered, Napoleon for the first time appeared to be refusing aid without a reasonable excuse. The Sardinian ambassador to Paris made more frequent and pointed remarks about the need for action against the Austrians as Cavour intensified pressure on Napoleon. His cousin, the Countess de Castiglione, appeared in Paris; and in moments of intimacy with the Emperor, she spoke of freeing Italy from Austria. While propaganda on this level did not move Napoleon, he was certainly disturbed by an attempt on his life on January 14, 1858, by Felice Orsini. Arrangements for the deed had been made in England, but the declared object was to destroy the man who had betrayed Italy. Napoleon's offers of exile were brusquely refused and Orsini was executed.

That one so close to Bonapartism as Orsini should have lost

faith in Napoleon was particularly upsetting. Also unnerving was his statement that though this particular plot failed, many other Italians were south of the Alps and eventually one would succeed in punishing the man who had turned his back on them. For whatever reason, sometime in the next few months Napoleon decided to make good on his pledge to "do something for Italy," and he arranged to meet Cavour to discuss details.

The two leaders met on July 21, 1858, at Plombières. Dressed as businessmen on vacation, they planned the expulsion of Austria from Italy while sitting at a table in a farmhouse. Cavour felt that he was humoring the Emperor's penchant for intrigue and secrecy and at the same time driving a hard bargain. Napoleon's foreign minister, Walewski, knew nothing of the meeting and its agreements. Many historians of the Empire have seen Napoleon's Italian involvement as a mistake and credited Cavour at Plombières as having outwitted the Emperor. To have taken Sardinia's side against Austria may have been an error, but it is now clear that Napoleon was not talked into this decision at Plombières. Indeed, Cavour did not change Napoleon's mind about any aspect of the entire project and was himself forced to make concessions.

Cavour was forced to carry back to his monarch word that the price of French aid would be the loss of Nice and Savoy, the ancestral home of the dynasty, as well as the marriage of his daughter, Chlotilde, to Prince Napoleon. Sardinia should arrange for a conflict with Austria in which Austria appeared the aggressor. France then would support both the principle of nationalities and the underdog. It was presumed that the other European powers would remain neutral, and that a quick campaign would expel Austria from Italy. The shape of the new Italy was not definitely agreed upon; both men were willing to see how events proceeded. Cavour's failure to accept completely Napoleon's scheme for a confederated Italy was really his only "triumph" at Plombières.

Victor Emmanuel accepted Napoleon's terms, and on January 26, 1859, a formal treaty was signed; its first result occurred four days later in Turin when Prince Napoleon married Chlotilde. From the Sardinian point of view arrangements had moved along satisfactorily and the expulsion of Austria could now take place.

In Paris Napoleon was beginning to temporize. He had encountered from his entourage an unexpected amount of hostility to further involvement in Italy. Walewski had furiously resigned when he learned of the arrangements made behind his back, and the generals were insisting that the army had not yet recovered from its exertions in the Crimea. At court the Emperor appeared virtually alone in his determination to help Italy, as even the Empress branded the venture as foolhardy. To his dismay only the republicans as a group were enthusiastic supporters of the adventure.

The powers of Europe sensed that a crisis over Italy was pending, and they were suspicious of Napoleon. He had taken steps to neutralize Russian apprehensions, but Prussia and England were becoming openly critical. Blunt Austrian demands on Sardinia, however, aided his stand, and Cavour seized the opportunity, goading Austria to war as an aggressor. On May 12, 1859, Napoleon entered Italy, ostensibly to defend an innocent, weak power being bullied by Austria. The Emperor of the French had embarked on a course that was to lead him from one insoluble problem to another, until at last his regime fell in 1870.

The army Napoleon commanded in Italy was barely adequate to the task. After its return from the Crimea, there had been no reorganization or attempts to correct serious deficiencies revealed late in the war. Though equal to the demands of Magenta and Solferino, it was a tired military instrument committed to a dangerous mission.

News that the French had entered northern Italy in force set off widespread insurrections in the rest of the peninsula. While the Emperor was leading his army to victory, he became increasingly apprehensive about events in central Italy. He suspected that Cavour was taking advantage of Austria's embarrassment to make a much more radical power adjustment than was mentioned at Plombières. Sardinia threatened to move into the vacancy left by Austria, resulting in a northern Italian kingdom of far greater proportions than Napoleon desired. The enlarged and ambitious Sardinia would endanger the other Italian states, including Papal holdings, and make unlikely the prospects of a workable confederation headed by the Pope.

Napoleon now conceived a new role for Austria in Italy. She was needed as a bulwark against further Sardinian growth and as a guarantor of the independence of much of Italy. Thus further conflict with Austria was senseless, and Napoleon arranged for an armistice on July 9 at Villafranca. Here the two emperors,

Francis Joseph and Napoleon, cordially met and agreed that Austria would cede Lombardy to France, who in turn ceded it to Sardinia. Venetia, however, was to be retained by Austria and the situation before the war was to be restored in other areas, especially in Modena and Tuscany. This was a bitter disappointment for Victor Emmanuel, but he showed more appreciation for the French position than Cavour, who resigned in outrage.

To Napoleon III, France had little reason for further hostilities against Austria, especially since Austria's forces were now in the famed Quadrilateral and future victories against them would be more difficult. Besides this new position of strength, Austria seemed to be France's best defense against the Prussian mobilization taking place along the Rhine. Two hundred thousand troops appeared poised for an invasion of France for which the Empire was unprepared.

Napoleon sought peace. He had, after all, "done something" for Italy. Sardinia was enlarged, and her domination of the rest of the peninsula proved largely a matter of time. By making a peace with Austria, which allowed her to still remain in Venetia, Napoleon had slowed the process of Italian unification and earned an attitude of wounded frustration on the part of many Italian radicals. He came out of the experience remarkably well-liked by the Austrians, who also viewed the Prussian mobilization with apprehension. While Sardinian domination of the peninsula was an objective of Victor Emmanuel's, it had never been a declared French or Napoleonic goal. Thus Napoleon could make peace in good conscience when French interests seemed to require it, regarding such a course as responsible leadership rather than treachery.

The war in Italy was not generally popular in France, nor were the terms of its settlement. Vocal Catholic critics were particularly alarmed by what appeared to be diminution of Papal power and prestige. Sardinia's new power was a threat to Rome, and Napoleon could only insist that French troops would always protect the Pope. That Austria had ceased to be a threat meant little in the face of the obvious stimulus to Italian nationalism that French arms in northern Italy had inspired. Formerly Napoleon had protected the Pope, but now he had clearly helped to endanger the Holy Father. By diminishing Austrian influence in Italy, he had opened the door to vast change that he could not control. Napoleon was disappointed that his efforts had not led to an Italian confederation led by the Pope, and he had not anticipated the loss of Catholic support in France.

Perhaps Napoleon III deserved better, since he really had been a friend of Rome and of Catholicism in France. During his presidency the Falloux Bill (1850) had given the Church its largest role in education since the Concordat. The expedition sent to Rome in 1849 to protect Pius IX still remained in Italy. At great expense France had supported Latin Christendom's demands in the dispute at Constantinople over the holy places. Catholic critics seemed to forget these acts in behalf of the Church as now they condemned his "meddling" in Italy.

Also alienated were French nationalists who would have preferred a war along the Rhine, but saw instead an inadequately defended frontier menaced by the Prussians. They also bemoaned the changes being made in Italy. Sardinia had been a third-rate state. Now, because of Napoleon, she was much stronger and was threatening to become a major power. Even worse, this new force bordering France was offended because of the terms of armistice with Austria at Villafranca. A weak state which could never have been a threat to France had been strengthened and transformed into a hostile neighbor.

Napoleon had expected gratitude from the Italians and assumed that Sardinia would be a French ally in future European diplomacy. In this, of course, he underrated the ambitions of Cavour and Victor Emmanuel. Nationalists in Italy believed he had betrayed them in their hour of greatest opportunity while nationalists in France charged that he had seriously endangered French security, both in Italy and along the Rhine.

The Emperor reacted to this criticism by increasing his demands on Victor Emmanuel for Nice and Savoy. After six months Cavour had returned to power and now tried to evade surrendering these areas to France. He argued that it had been agreed Nice and Savoy were to go to France if the Austrians were driven from Italy. The terms of Villafranca, however, allowed the Austrians to remain in Venetia, and so the French had not kept their bargain and were not entitled to Nice and Savoy. But Napoleon was determined, and French pressure was too strong for Cavour. Plebiscites in Nice and Savoy overwhelmingly supported the transfer from Sardinian to French sovereignty, which occurred late in April, 1860, accompanied by a wave of genuine enthusiasm for Napoleon. Cavour then insisted that Sardinia needed compensation for giving up these territories and Napoleon did nothing to prevent his making significant accretions to the Sardinian state in Tuscany, Modena and Parma. French borders had been extended, the first such alteration since 1815, but at a cost of further strengthening Sardinia and endangering the Papacy. Welcome as Nice and Savoy were, the critics of the Emperor's policies in Italy remained unsatisfied.

This Italian campaign left Sardinia enlarged but offended, Austria resigned but irritated and Prussia highly suspicious of the French; it also left other powers feeling endangered. Switzerland was especially disturbed by the transfer of Savoy and used her diplomacy to oppose the French designs. She saw her own defensive situation markedly less secure and spread an alarm warning against the aggressive pattern of French expansion.

The English had been suspicious of Napoleon's invasion of northern Italy, but were prepared to accept the humbling of Austria as essential to legitimate Sardinian interests. They were ready to welcome the defeat of reactionary princes in Italy, but were incensed when Napoleon insisted on Nice and Savoy as a reward for his services. It proved to them that this maker of coups was the scheming manipulator they had suspected all along.

To appease the English, Napoleon could point to a remarkable commercial document, the Cobden-Chevalier Treaty of January 23, 1860. In it the Emperor committed France to a drastic reduction of tariffs in her trade with England—explicit evidence of Napoleon's liberal ideas in commerce and trade. Ironically for Napoleon, this treaty failed to win him much respect in Britain, where his motives were always suspect. The English were consistently impervious to favors from Napoleon, whether they be French lives given manning English trenches in the Crimea or commercial profits. At the same time the treaty alienated many important French industrialists. The reduced rates were probably set too low initially and British manufactured goods, especially textiles and iron products, flooded French markets, forcing many marginal producers out of business. Protectionism had been a way of life for French businessmen; now many were exposed to vigorous competition. The immediate result was a chorus of criticism; the long-term result was a healthier and better organized productive capacity. (The Emperor, however, did not live long enough to enjoy much praise for his enlightened economic policies.) The railway investors whose lines Napoleon had protected by going into Italy were now his critics. The only compensation was an increased British sale of French silks, wines and brandies, but again the rates were too low. Thus he had alienated significant segments of the business community with no appreciable personal gain, either in France or England.

Napoleon's negotiation of the Cobden-Chevalier treaty while he was suspiciously involved in Italian affairs assured a measure of misunderstanding. The treaty was recognized as reflecting his Saint-Simonian leanings. He soon negotiated similar treaties with Belgium, Switzerland and the German Zollverein. While these treaties seemed to indicate an economic liberalism and faith in free trade, the context in which they occurred suggested that they were merely a political gambit: the Emperor was simply trying to win back support lost in Italy. Nearly everything constructive that Napoleon attempted was surrounded by the same suspicion. While it is tempting to conclude that he never received adequate credit for being responsible or conscientious, his actions were usually politically motivated. His involvement in Italy was a great mistake, but could he have avoided it? Once committed, should he have gone to Villafranca? Could his army have sustained much more campaigning? These are questions with no answers, but out of the whole situation a weakened Emperor emerged. From this point on, each action would be tainted with the suspicion that he was simply trying to win back the support of some previously alienated group.

By 1860 opposition to the government within France was recognizable and articulate. Its formal emergence dated from the 1857 elections to the Legislative Body when 750,000 votes were cast for opposition candidates. These votes, signalling a substantial disenchantment with the Empire, were cast mostly in Paris, but also in Lyons, Marsailles and Bordeaux. Elected in Paris were Carnot and Goudchaux, who refused to take the oath, and Cavaignac, who died shortly thereafter. Representatives of the capital who were finally seated were republicans Jules Favre, Ernest Picard, Jacques-Louis Henon, Emile Ollivier and L.-Alfred Darimon. Ollivier was the spokesman of this group, known as "The Five," which became the core of opposition to the government. Though their numbers were soon to grow, for a time they played only a minor role, being virtually ignored during proceedings.

There had been continuous opposition to Napoleon, dating from the beginning of his presidency. The republicans were annoyed when the new chief executive selected as his first ministers men with strong Orleanist leanings (after Lamartine refused to serve). The republicans were unable to organize effectively, however, and the coup drove them either underground or into exile. A vigorous censorship of the press resulted in a muzzling of republican publications. As under Charles X and Louis Philippe in his later days, the result was a smattering of anonymous tracts and a flowering of literary and philosophical journals which the government properly viewed with extreme suspicion. After the election of 1857, the republican position could be moderately articulated in the Legislative Body, and republicans girded themselves for the next major electoral contests.

The Catholic opposition, likewise, had its roots in Napoleon's presidency. As the *Union électorale* they constituted a kind of political party whose leaders met regularly at an address in the Rue de Poitiers. This was a disparate group which shared a common belief in the importance of a strong church. Its members supported Napoleon for several years, but by 1860 they became part of a vigorous Catholic opposition. Catholic leaders became critics in a number of non-church questions where they found ready allies among republicans, disaffected Orleanists, nationalists and protectionists. The growing cohesiveness and enlargement of groups opposing the Emperor made a reconsideration of the bases of his power expedient, leading him *perhaps* to a decision to bid openly for liberal support. In this light the trade treaties were a bold request for new assistance and have been regarded by one writer as constituting a fiscal coup d'état against the established economic order.

In April, 1859, Napoleon granted a general amnesty to all political exiles, allowing them to return to France. Instead of winning republican gratitude, the measure resulted in their increased agitation and a more vigorous republican press. When the government shut down the papers and prosecuted their journalists, a forum was created for republican lawyers like Leon Gambetta to attack both imperial restrictions and institutions. Among the critics of the regime after 1859 was Adolphe Thiers, who provided vocal leadership for a group of Orleanists. Thus by mid-1860 a number of eloquent spokesmen critical of the Empire had appeared and could not be ignored.

After careful consideration Napoleon decided to make major concessions to "the parties." These were embodied in the Decrees of November 24, 1860, and constituted the beginnings of what has been called the Liberal Empire. Napoleon reminded France of his promise to "crown the edifice with liberty" after coming to power, while assuring stability and order. Had he begun this move prior to the elections of 1857 or before his involvement in Italy in 1859, his claim that his motivation for liberalizing the regime was altruistic would have appeared more credible. As it was, the granting of increased political rights looked like merely another political gambit.

Among those advising liberalization was Morny. He believed that if the developing opposition groups were openly allowed to give advice, perpetual disagreement and strife among the parties would result. The Emperor could then pose as a wise mediator, taking credit for successes while the "politicians" could be blamed for mistakes. For Morny, at least, the concessions were a matter of Machiavellian logic rather than any belief in republican principles. How much Napoleon was swayed by such thinking is an open question. He was Machiavellian, to be sure, but he was also a Forty-eighter and the bearer of a romantic legend.

The Decrees allowed the Legislative Body to present an annual address to the Emperor, and sessions were open to the public. Its proceedings were to be published in greater detail. The beginnings of a parliamentary regime had thus been established, and it was probably as genuine a product as those that controlled France between 1815 and 1848. Liberalization of press restrictions in the spring of 1861 brought praise from Ollivier but worried many republicans. The Emperor appeared to be slowly putting into effect much of the substance of the republican program. Questions abounded about the wisdom of the liberalization and its effect on the Emperor's popularity. An indication of how extensive the opposition had become was demonstrated in 1863 when thirty-five opposition candidates, seventeen of them republican, were elected to the Legislative Body with the help of 2,000,000 votes. The election had been hard-fought, with critics of the regime combining to work against government candidates. Napoleon attributed a large part of the hostile vote to blunders on Persigny's part. This devoted but short-sighted minister had waged a tactless campaign which surely cost the government some support. Still the vote for official candidates topped 5,300,000, and the opinion of some zealots that the Empire was falling was clearly premature.

Among the new faces in the Legislative Body was Thiers, who soon delivered a major pronouncement. In a speech on January 11, 1864, he in effect offered a reconciliation to the Emperor. Entitling his remarks "On Necessary Liberties," he listed the price for which he would willingly become an obedient and grateful citizen of the Empire. He wanted free elections, free national representation, freedom of the press save for slander, personal freedom from violence and arbitrary arrest, and he wanted majority public opinion to direct the government. All of this meant ministerial responsibility, the end of official candidates and the repeal of the law of public safety. His tone was somber and deferential, but he could not resist noting that if the changes he desired were not made, the time would come when the country would demand them.

This offer from one of the country's most alert politicians has been presented as a rare opportunity for the Emperor to win his adherence. However, the price was high for the time, and Napoleon declined. Speaking for the government, Rouher declared that antiquated notions of constitutionality were no reason to hand the throne over to the unhealthy passions of a parliamentary regime. Thiers' response was a cutting observation that the only antiquated notion was despotism.

Could an accommodation with Thiers have been achieved in 1864? Considering Thiers' volatile character, it is an open question whether such a partnership could have worked for long. While Ollivier and others might have at once cooperated with the Emperor, would such independent personalities as Gambetta, Favre and Picard? Since Napoleon did ultimately come close to accepting many of Thiers' ideas, what he really missed was a chance to speed up the liberalization. It would have looked like an admission of weakness after the 1863 elections, but—in light of the future—France would have had several years' experience with her new parliamentary regime before the supreme test of 1870. By moving slowly, however, the Emperor would be able to see whether the opposition, whose numbers had only now become significant in the Legislative Body, would be truly constructive or simply dedicated to grasping more power. After 1859 virtually every concession granted by the Emperor was used against the regime. And, after all, by what right did Thiers think he could make demands or offers to the Emperor? In reality he proposed a sort of blackmail. Napoleon was told at what price Thiers would become a loyal citizen, but the old Orleanist overrated his nuisance value. Had further liberalization not occurred or had the Empire fallen because it had not liberalized (or if Thiers had been responsible for either of these), then it would be appropriate to regard the Emperor's rejection of Thiers' offer as a tragic mistake. As it was, when particular demands for liberalization were not met, opposition lines merely hardened and prepared to continue embarrassing the regime. The Authoritarian Empire, with its docile, cooperative Legislative Body and subservient ministries, had ended. Now the government's voice was not the only voice as the tempo of political life quickened under the Liberal Empire.

Imperial Triumphs and Frustrations in the Sixties

As indicated earlier, the conquest of Algeria was well under way when Louis Napoleon was elected to the presidency. There remained pockets of resistance, but these were gradually reduced. By 1857 the conquest was complete, boundaries were secure and Europeans encouraged to colonize. For a short time the authority of the army in Algeria was reduced while Napoleon allowed Prince Napoleon to govern Algeria, through a bureau within the ministry of the interior. He dropped this plan and restored the army to its dominant role when the Algerians proved to have little respect for prefects and Prince Napoleon showed little interest. Meanwhile the Algerian economy made great strides as European methods and products were successfully introduced.

In 1860 Napoleon and the Empress made a trip to Algeria for a firsthand view of the land. Napoleon returned much impressed with the colony's potential, and especially concerned about the status of the Arab population. After considerable thought he wrote to Marshal Pelissier, then governor general, that Algeria was "not properly speaking a colony" but "an Arab kingdom." He concluded: "The natives have the same right to my protection as European colonists. I am Emperor of the Arabs the way I am Emperor of the French." This was an intriguing application of the principle of nationalities to which he fervently subscribed. It led him to favor special territorial arrangements along tribal lines for the natives, with the idea of keeping them from being forced to accept European customs regarding property rights. These ideas were never taken very seriously by army men and bureaucrats in Algeria, so the Algerians did not realize the extent of the Emperor's efforts in their interests. Sporadic insurrections against French rule broke out in 1864, requiring a major effort to restore order. The next year Napoleon again visited Algeria (accompanied by Margaret Bellanger), issuing pardons to the tribes recently in revolt and promising them more of a share in the administration of the area, including more equitable taxes and more public works. The result was a tumultuous outpouring of Arab sentiment for the Emperor, who was praised as a magnanimous conqueror. In his entire career Napoleon never received more emotional or impressive acclaim than on his second visit to Algeria.

While Algeria was adjusting to the influx of thousands of European settlers, a French foothold in Senegal was being extended. In 1850 France maintained a series of trading posts at the sufferance of the native Moors and Toucouleurs, who exacted regular blackmail payments. Napoleon enlarged the garrison, and under Captain (later General) Faidherbe the area was pacified by 1858. Peace was made with tribal chieftains, and the Senegalese basin was brought under French sovereignty. From there approaches were made to the chieftains of the Niger. These developments were accelerated after the fall of Napoleon III and led ultimately to the establishment of French West Africa.

While the Empire was laying firm foundations in Africa, it also embarked on a remarkable venture in Southeast Asia. French missionaries and merchants had been in the Far East for over a decade, but their activities were negligible compared with British interests, which were substantial and of long standing. While trying to placate England over the Italian campaign by negotiating the Cobden-Chevalier treaty, Napoleon also agreed to cooperate with the English in their smouldering dispute with China, sending out a naval expeditionary force with 8,000 volunteer troops commanded by General Cousin-Montauban.

The Chinese were technologically unprepared for the forces facing them. On September 21, 1860, 40,000 of their cavalry were unable to disperse 800 French troops at Palikao. While aiding Britain against China, the French became embroiled in Cochin China where Christians worshipped only with great difficulty and harrassment. French naval demonstrations and military units were initially dispatched to force a conference which would assure

Christians the right of worship. In June, 1862, the result was a cession to France of all lower Cochin China and the establishment of a protectorate over Cambodia. An unsuccessful rebellion left the French in control over all of Cochin China. This foothold in Asia was accomplished without design and at little expense on the part of Napoleon, who never took it very seriously, thinking of it mainly as a trading station. After the fall of the Empire it was to be an object of major French colonial activity in the East.

Another movement of French troops was a matter of considerable diplomatic anxiety. Some 7,000 men commanded by General d'Haut-poul landed in Syria in August of 1860. The occasion was the "Syrian Massacres," which had stirred all of Christian Europe. In a three-day period 5,000 Christians were killed as anti-Christian violence and murder went unchecked. Ottoman authorities did nothing to protect their Christian subjects, and the British and French, the powers that barely five years before had defended the Turks, now became alarmed. Still apprehensive about Napoleonic designs, the English grudgingly agreed to the offer that French troops be sent representing the Western powers. Once the French had landed, the Turks held a few summary trials in a show of justice. Most of the murderers went unpunished, but the massacres did end and Christian rights were protected by a new constitutional arrangement for Lebanon. The French force withdrew on June 5, 1861, their mission accomplished. A long-range result was a residual prestige for France in Lebanon and other Christian communities in the Near East. In the short run, despite France's trade treaty with England, despite her help against China and her support of the English cause in Syria, Napoleon still failed to gain the trust and confidence of officials in London.

Under Napoleon III France was involved in another Middle East venture of particular long-range significance, the opening of the Suez Canal in 1869. This was the achievement largely of Ferdinand de Lesseps, a cousin of the Empress who had served as a French consul in Cairo. Both the Empress and the Emperor gave enthusi-astic support to de Lesseps. They lent their prestige to his efforts to float bonds, and gave money themselves. The Emperor was espe-cially interested in the Suez project; in his military studies he had pondered the impact on world trade of canals in strategic places. At Ham he had devised a plan for a canal through Nicaragua. De Lesseps solved the host of diplomatic, political, administrative, legal, fiscal and engineering problems involved and, after ten years of construction, the canal was opened. In 1869, although the Emperor was ill and the Empire was unsuspectingly near its death agony, the completion of the canal was the occasion for a spectacular and nearly universal outpouring of public praise for de Lesseps, for the Empress and for France. Eugénie traveled to Egypt for the formal opening. An armada of forty-eight warships from all nations welcomed her with countless salutes. Minor princes, ministers and ambassadors were present, along with the Prince and Princess of Holland, the Prince Royal of Prussia and Emperor Francis Joseph of Austria. Even Abd-el-Kader, the wily Arab chieftain who had fought France in Algeria and rested in her prisons, was there. It was surely one of the Empire's finest moments.

In 1861 Napoleon once more participated in a cooperative venture with the English. This time the outcome was to be tragic for the Emperor and the Empire. Along with Spain, France and England signed the London Agreement on October 31, 1861; the idea was to send a joint military expedition to Mexico to force its new liberal government, headed by Juárez, to honor its debts to foreign nationals. Cooperation among the three powers soon succumbed to jealousies and conflicting motives, destroying the alliance within six months. By May, 1862, the English and Spanish had both abandoned the enterprise, but Napoleon had by then sent to Mexico about 7,000 men who were moving against Juárez. A French defeat at Puebla on May 5, 1862, called attention not only to the French efforts against Juárez, but also to the fact that though the defeated force was small, it was the first major loss of French arms in the field in more than a decade. This provoked the Emperor to quickly add 23,000 men to his forces in Mexico. With General E. F. Forey in command, Puebla was finally taken more than a year later, and on June 7, 1863, the French marched into Mexico City. Shortly thereafter the Austrian archduke, Maximilian, brother of Francis Joseph, was established under French auspices as the Emperor of Mexico. By this time Napoleon had completely forfeited English support and respect. He had proven himself, in their view, as unreliable as they had suspected earlier, in the Syrian affair.

In this Mexican venture we see Napoleon III as his opponents generally conceived him—the Machiavellian plotter par excellence. Mexico exercised a strong hold over his imagination. He imagined her as a rejuvenated Latin Catholic power, a bulwark against the southward expansion of the Protestant United States. He again recalled the commercial advantages of a canal through Nicaragua and began to think in terms of a vast Central American empire. The Empress was even more emotional about the prospects. As a Spaniard she wanted to see liberal and independent Mexico crushed, and as a devout Catholic she wanted to see the conservative elements in society restored. Juárez's rival, Miramon, had a spokesman at the court in Paris, General Almonte, who particularly impressed the Empress by his pleas.

Napoleon weighed other considerations, concluding that the United States was so fully engaged in its civil war that it was unlikely to play any significant role in Mexican affairs for some time. (Like the English, he supported the South, an embarrassing circumstance when it lost its struggle.) Establishing Maximilian as emperor seemed a fitting gesture to win Austria's friendship after restricting her power in Italy. Italy was still pressing Napoleon to arrange a cession of Venetia, and the thought that Austria would welcome such a transfer, as a gesture of thanks for setting up Maximilian, was a factor in his thinking. As for the Church, he hoped that the Papacy and Catholics in France might be pleased.

All these ideas swirled through Napoleon's mind as he listened to the pleas of French businessmen asking protection for their investments. Morny and others had lent vast sums to Miramon, and they were demanding that Juárez be made to pay. The Emperor probably made the worst decision of his career in deciding to control Mexico. It proved to be a vastly expensive and dismal failure. The result was humiliating and exposed the regime to acid criticism from its opponents.

What went wrong? Virtually everything. The popular support for Juárez in Mexico was never properly understood by Napoleon. Ironically, the army performed its task well, especially after Bazaine replaced Forey, and Juárez was driven into hiding.

Attempts to establish a proper civil government were only partially successful. Maximilian had been advised by Napoleon to put himself at the head of the masses; but instead he at once sympathized with the conservative aristocracy and clergy. Probably no Hapsburg could really understand the idea of being a spokesman for the lower classes of a population. Even so, he quarreled with the clergy over the ownership of Church lands, thus alienating the Church without winning any liberal or popular support. In addition, after the civil war in the United States had ended with a Union victory, the government in Washington adopted a menacing posture, openly supporting Juárez. Tax collections in Mexico were never adequate, and as expenses mounted and one difficulty after another arose, Napoleon decided to withdraw his troops. Maximilian was quarreling with Bazaine, furious at not being better supported by the French Emperor, who, after all, had promised him an army of 25,000 men until 1867 and the Foreign Legion until 1873. Early in 1866, Napoleon explicitly instructed Bazaine to make appropriate preparations to leave. After Sadowa Maximilian was advised to abdicate, but he believed that he enjoyed enough of a following to survive without the French. Bazaine left Mexico City on February 5, 1867; his withdrawal was orderly. With the French army gone, Maximilian was quickly captured by Juárez and executed. The whole episode was a disaster, and critics in France rightly deplored the loss of both prestige and money.

While the Mexican venture was running its course, Napoleon's diplomacy in Europe suffered a series of reverses. The center of his attention was drawn to north central Europe where Bismarck's Prussia was embarking on a new, militaristic program. The Emperor had liked Bismarck and had regarded Prussia with favor, as a sort of Sardinia of the north. Frequent insurrections in Poland, starting in 1861 and lasting into 1863, put Napoleon in a difficult position. As a friend of nationalities and protector of small states, many expected him to come to the aid of the Poles. However, this would have jeopardized the friendship he enjoyed with Alexander II. His temporizing was strongly criticized within France, but his only response, other than expressions of sympathy for the Poles, was to suggest a general European conference to discuss the major problems of the continent. He was rebuffed by the English, while Bismarck gained Russia's friendship by closing Prussian borders to Poles attempting to escape from the Tsar's repression.

Close on the heels of the Polish problem came a reopening of the Schleswig-Holstein question and an Austro-Prussian attack on Denmark in February, 1864. Napoleon had remonstrated but sent no troops while the Poles were being crushed; now he similarly did nothing while the Danes were being defeated. The English proposed joint action with France, but the Emperor declined, fearing an attack on the Rhine. He candidly explained to Clarendon that he was not ready for war, and so the new Austro-Prussian administration of Schleswig and Holstein simply had to be accepted.

Prussian mobilization along the Rhine in 1859 had made Napoleon very sensitive about this frontier. He regarded an accretion of Prussian territory to be appropriate—he still thought of Austria as a reactionary state—and so he favored an enlarged German state formed around a Prussian nucleus. He considered that a struggle between Prussia and Austria might be necessary, but saw no threat to France in such a conflict. He recognized that the changes going on in Germany might afford opportunities for a transfer of Venetia to Italy and for a French satellite buffer state along the Rhine. The Emperor expected France to profit from any basic changes in central Europe.

In October, 1864 and 1865, the Emperor met with Bismarck at Biarritz for conversations about Germany, which have been as ambiguously recorded as those of Plombières. Bismarck left with a feeling that while Napoleon wanted French influence increased along the Rhine, he would do nothing in case of a struggle between Austria and Prussia. From Napoleon's insistence that Austria transfer Venetia to Italy came a provision for an Italo-Prussian alliance should war break out within three months. Austria also approached Napoleon and for his assurances of neutrality in the coming struggle promised to give up Venetia. On the surface of things the Emperor seemed to be in a strong position. By diplomacy alone he had guaranteed the transfer of Venetia. In a drawn-out struggle between Prussia and Austria, he expected to mediate a settlement that would place him again in a position as arbiter of Europe and result in French gains along the Rhine.

The stunning defeat of Austria at Sadowa (Königgrätz) on July 3, 1866, completely upset most of his calculations. Austria had fought alone against Prussia and Italy, handily defeating the Italians. Austrian failure before the new Prussian army amazed virtually all observers; but then, it was Napoleon in 1859 who had demonstrated Austrian weakness to the world. Napoleon belatedly offered mediation but was politely disregarded by Bismarck. The Prussian statesman similarly evaded his demands for compensation, and he was little more than an observer to the creation of the North German Confederation in 1867. The defeat of the Austrians at Sadowa was widely regarded as a serious diplomatic setback for Napoleon—indeed he was as much a victim as the Austrians—and within France a torrent of criticism was directed against the Emperor's conduct of foreign affairs.

In 1866 Napoleon inspired more complaints when he negotiated the temporary withdrawal of the French garrison from Rome on condition that Italy not move on the Pope. This arrangement lasted only ten months. Besides earning bitter criticism from Catholics within France, it hastened the Papal issuance of the encyclical *Quanta cura,* with its famous appendix, *Syllabus errorum,* which were, in part, attacks on the French regime.

After some thought about his predicament—the Mexican disaster was omnipresent and his health was swiftly deteriorating—the Emperor announced a further liberalizing of the Empire. With considerable fanfare, a few modest changes were made. Now ministers could be questioned from the floor of the Legislative Body and laws could be examined in detail. The Senate assumed a legislative function, so that effectively there were two legislative houses. There was a liberalizing of regulations about public assembly, and press restrictions were to be loosened.

These changes won him little sympathy. He merely lost some conservative support without winning over republicans or liberals, who continued to criticize the Mexican fiasco and remind France of the danger of an enlarged Prussia. News of Maximilian's death on June 19 with Miramon by his side merely emphasized the sense of French failure.

The test of these reforms would be reflected in the sort of men the Emperor appointed in his new cabinet, and when most of the same faces (Rouher, Duruy, La Valette, Baroche) reappeared, without Ollivier or another republican, Thiers quickly branded it all a hoax. Even as events were turning against the Emperor, he was not yet ready to yield to the uproar. He was still in control and asserted that he intended to liberalize at his own speed and in his own good time.

The Liberal Empire and Its Demise

The triumphal opening of the Suez Canal was 1869's only major success for Napoleon III. Otherwise it was a year that saw more failures of French leadership heaped upon the twin disasters of the Prussian victory at Sadowa and Maximilian's execution. The Emperor had tried to counteract the growth of Prussian influence in central Europe by belatedly claiming that compensation for France was essential to maintain the balance of power. Bismarck refused to consider German land along the Rhine but encouraged Napoleon to believe that possibly some arrangements might be made regarding Luxembourg and Belgium. After French designs on these territories were put in writing, the Prussian statesman quietly allowed negotiations to die.

Napoleon, however, was anxious for some sort of accretion to French territory and sensed an opportunity to simply purchase Luxembourg. Its grand duke, the King of Holland, was willing to sell, and Bismarck hinted that it was perfectly feasible if done quietly and quickly. News of the scheme leaked (from Bismarck?), and the Dutch monarch changed his mind. An international congress in London in May, 1867, emphasized the grand duchy's neutrality in international affairs, and its ties with Prussia and the Germanic Confederation were severed. The French Emperor stood exposed as a shabby plotter, his foreign policy further discredited.

The apprehensions aroused over the Luxembourg incident had hardly died when another embarrassing episode occurred. A French railroad company had leased two Belgian lines, and it looked to critics like a Napoleonic attempt to move on Belgium through economic means. Again the foreign and republican press branded the Emperor a scheming and untrustworthy neighbor. Belgian statesmen sought to get out of the arrangement and were supported by Prussia and Great Britain. Napoleon was irritated and speculated testily that the Belgians were now arrogant because they thought Prussia would protect them but when honor was involved, war could come. He finally backed down but still tried to get an alliance with the Belgians. Supported by both Berlin and London, the government in Brussels refused, so that Napoleon was even denied a graceful withdrawal from this sticky situation. The criticism from this episode was widespread in the early months of 1869. The year saw the Empire mercilessly attacked and openly rejected by an increasing number of people.

The opposition press had grown substantially during the previous decade while the number of government-controlled papers had declined. Several of the new journals were especially forthright in their condemnation of the regime. Despotism was a term they commonly applied to this system—a system that was tolerating their complaints. Victor Hugo authored especially intemperate attacks in *Le Rappel*, but perhaps the most telling of the Empire's detractors was Henri Rochefort. Lampooning the Emperor in *La Lanterne*, he penned the widely quoted witticism that France had 36,000,000 subjects, not counting those of discontent. Republican firebrand Leon Gambetta was now insisting on much more than Thiers wanted in 1864 and

more than most republicans even hoped for in 1869. He was calling
for separation of church and state, elections for all public officials,
free and universal compulsory secular education and suppression of
the standing army. Vigorous as all these critics were, nearly all had
accepted the dynasty. The main object of their complaints was only
to get a more liberal and responsible government.

In this atmosphere of public censure and complaint, May elections
were held and most of the candidates for seats in the Legislative
Body publicly sympathized with Gambetta's opposition to a standing army. About 45 per cent or nearly 3,500,000 people voted for
opposition candidates, while the official government candidates received a majority of less than a million votes. It was a stunning
rebuke.

While the Emperor debated what to do, his close friend of many
years, Marshal Niel, died. Morny had passed away some years before and Napoleon himself was in almost constant pain. It was clear
that the control of affairs had to be passed to another generation.
Napoleon's problem was how to do it. As Ollivier had told him, "It
will take men of the rising generation to save Your Majesty's son."

Persigny had been dropped from his post as minister of the interior after playing an inept role in the 1863 elections, but he had
continued to give advice. He now urged immediate liberalization,
while the minister of state, Eugène Rouher, and the Empress were
for standing firm, making limited concessions at most. The Emperor
decided to liberalize further—in effect dropping Rouher—and to
allow Ollivier to form a ministry enjoying the confidence of the Legislative Body. Ollivier had become a favorite of the Emperor, but as
final negotiations with him were proceeding, Napoleon was dis-
mayed to realize that Ollivier really was a loner—he led no faction
and could not guarantee a specific number of votes when needed.
Further, Ollivier was adamant on the inclusion in his cabinet of two
old Orleanists, Napoleon Daru and Louis-Joseph Buffet.

After some debate, the Emperor gave way. The alternative to
Ollivier, after all, appeared to be Thiers, whom Napoleon had come
to regard as an unacceptable, personal enemy. But Thiers could
create a strong government. At this point Thiers was willing to support Ollivier, whom he saw as a man who would very much need his
assistance. Thiers' thinking was much the same as in late 1848.

On New Year's Day of 1870, Napoleon III decreed the establishment of ministerial responsibility. The Legislative Body could now

bring down the ministry, but no solution was offered for a possible deadlock between Emperor and legislature. France had returned to 1848. Again, the granting of reform appeared forced, so that while the Emperor this time received a measure of praise and public thanks from many politicians, it was inadequate recognition for the enormity of the change.

A plebiscite was planned for May, 1870, to determine whether or not the people approved all the constitutional alterations made since 1860. Many republicans worked diligently to increase the opposition vote over that of 1869, but the result was a resounding victory for the Emperor. Three million more people supported the regime than had the year before. The Emperor was delighted with the so-called renewal of the lease, and Ollivier and others assured him that he now could cease to worry about the dynasty. "We will arrange a comfortable old age for the Emperor," declared Ollivier.

Napoleon had rescued France from the chaos of 1848, broken the 1815 restrictions on France, restored the nation to a position of prominence in Europe and now given her enlightened institutions. But his sense of final triumph, after the despair of 1869, was to be short lived. The system he had so painfully evolved was cut short by military defeat.

Spanish nationalism had played a large part in the fall of Napoleon Bonaparte; it was perhaps fitting that the specific crisis leading to the end of the Second Empire had its origin in Spain. After 1815 that unhappy land had seen dynastic civil war and bitter political struggles. Queen Isabella II supported absolutist policies and led a life of moral turpitude and scandal. Revolts and insurrections were common, and in September, 1868, she was overthrown. A provisional government was formed with authority centered in a rebellious officer, General Prim.

To the embarrassment and frustration of Napoleon III, Isabella sought haven in France. Napoleon now had to be more concerned about French defenses in the Pyrenees. Further, her exile had ended discussions of Spanish troops' replacing the French in protecting the Pope. All told, it amounted to a lessening of French security; it also meant that French leaders would be acutely interested in Isabella's successor.

In Madrid the provisional government considered a number of possible candidates and in due course offered the crown to Prince Leopold of Hohenzollern-Sigmaringen, a young prince whose brother had received Napoleon's support in becoming King Carol of Rumania. Bismarck was in close contact with General Prim and played a significant part in Leopold's nomination.

The news of Leopold as prospective king of Spain touched off a general storm of indignation in Paris. Republicans, such as Gambetta and Favre, were in agreement with Thiers and Bonapartists that to have a Hohenzollern on the throne south of the Pyrenees was utterly unacceptable, and that unless Leopold's nomination was declined, war with Prussia was the only course consistent with French honor. They believed that King William of Prussia, as head of the Hohenzollern house, should be held responsible if Leopold accepted the post. Though alarmed at the developing crisis, Napoleon was impressed with the widespread unanimity evident in Paris. While he and the ministry worked to lessen the crisis, French newspapers were at fever pitch in calling for war. A nationalistic fervor spread rapidly, and converts to a war policy soon included the Empress and members of the ministry.

To the relief of the Emperor, Leopold explicitly declined the opportunity to mount the Spanish throne. This had been the advice of King William, who was annoyed over the whole episode. When William learned of Leopold's decision, he was as relieved as anyone that the issue seemed resolved. To Napoleon it also appeared that war had been avoided, and the general appearance was of a French diplomatic triumph.

In Paris, unfortunately, a number of zealots regarded the victory as inadequate. They wanted Prussia to be openly humiliated, a Sadowa in reverse. Among this group were the foreign minister (the Duke of Gramont), Gambetta and the Empress. On July 12 Gramont composed a telegram requesting Count Benedetti, the ambassador to Prussia, to approach King William, then vacationing at Ems, for assurance that the candidacy would not be renewed. None of the other ministers had been consulted about the telegram, but Napoleon allowed its transmission. This act made Napoleon partly to blame for the war and set off the chain of events that gave Bismarck another opportunity to foment hostilities after his earlier efforts had been foiled.

At Ems the French ambassador and the Prussian monarch had earlier conferred, and on receiving Gramont's telegram Benedetti quickly conveyed its substance to William. The King had by now privately urged the withdrawal of the candidacy and was to write reassuringly to Napoleon. However, he was irritated at the informality and irregularity of this latest meeting (in a park), and after refusing to discuss the subject further, he reported the incident by telegram to Bismarck at Berlin. This wily statesman altered the wording of the telegram to sharpen the episode, making it appear that a blunt and impertinent ultimatum had been refused by the King. The press eagerly published this version, known to history as the "Ems dispatch."

In the Paris press news of the Ems dispatch inspired more intemperate and warlike editorials. This time, however, a few calm heads, among them Thiers', observed that now there was no adequate cause for war. But emotions had risen sharply and few people even cared to wait for Benedetti's return from Ems. Bismarck's treachery could have been exposed, to the propaganda benefit of France. Throughout the crisis Gramont and the Empress were consistently militant, while Napoleon seemed fearful of war but ready to countenance it if need be.

Serious errors of judgment were made by all of the French leaders; yet history must not forget that the real fomenter of war in 1870 was Otto von Bismarck. Technically, the French made the initial declaration of war on July 19. It was a tragic mistake for France, prompted by a host of misconceptions. In addition to the public's being misinformed about the Ems dispatch, Napoleon III overrated the prospects that a war with Prussia would find both Italy and Austria by his side. His war minister, Le Boeuf, was reassuring, and the other ministers presumed that hostilities with Prussia would see a French army move rapidly across the Rhine into South Germany, campaigning in concert with Austria and Italy. South Germany would become a sort of base area from which the French would move out against Prussia.

The French had misread the situation completely. The Ems episode created opinion favorable to Prussia in South Germany, where the French declaration of war appeared as a threat. This provided Bismarck with the sense of urgency and cohesiveness in the south that he needed to make unified action possible. Meanwhile, he had publicized Napoleon's 1866 demand for Belgium, isolating the French Emperor from any remote possibility of English aid. Prussia had been a lenient victor in 1866, and in 1870 Austria was apprehensive about supporting the nation who had beaten her in Italy. More important, perhaps, her lingering ambitions to recoup her prestige in

Germany could not be realized in alliance with France, especially in view of the publicity over Napoleonic designs on his neighbors, Luxembourg and Belgium. Had the French won some initial victories, however, Austria might have joined them for opportunistic reasons. As it was, to ally with Italy was distasteful to her, she felt weakened by the *Ausgleich* and was, with Bismarck's blessing, beginning to look avariciously to Ottoman territories. On July 20, the Austrian government decided on neutrality; but its minister to France, Prince Metternich, later wrote to Le Boeuf that he hoped to provide France with "a nice little reinforcement of 300,000 men."

Italy recognized an obligation to France, but could not welcome an alliance with Austria and was more interested in having French troops leave Rome. Victor Emmanuel personally wanted to aid Napoleon, but in this he was quite alone. He was even ready to march with Austria. His foreign minister, Visconti-Venosta, tried to avert war through organizing a league of neutrals. But he failed in his efforts, partly because the French seemed bent on war. Hurried negotiations resulted in an Austro-Italian agreement to temporary neutrality while they made preparations to enter the war as allies of France. French defeats were to nullify prospects of this aid.

France's greatest misconception concerned the condition of her army. In July the war minister, Le Boeuf, saw no problems. He described the army as prepared and superior to that of Prussia. He felt that it would require only two weeks to have 300,000 men ready, and another 100,000 within call. This confident talk was assuring to those who wanted war; but, barely ten weeks before, he had described the "German" army as having "1,140,000 trained and disciplined men" while the French could "throw not more than 510,000 men into our battle line."

The army had, in fact, not been kept up-to-date since the campaign in Italy. Responsibility lay with the Emperor for not *insisting*, during the sixties, on modernization and on more money for the army. Marshal Niel had been most emphatic on the need for reform, and Napoleon had made appropriate recommendations for funds; but when these were refused or cut back in the Legislative Body, he acquiesced. This was perhaps the price of liberalism and too much attention to critics.

During the 1860's the army took part in many minor expeditions. However, these never required full-scale commitments and the Emperor appeared reluctant to engage in a major war. Thus Sadowa revealed far more than merely a tactical error by Napoleon. Why did he so studiously avoid going to war at that time? The idea that he could not fight because of the troops in Mexico is unsound since the numbers committed to Mexico were never very large, not enough in themselves to influence events in Europe. Napoleon knew that his army was unprepared; philosophically, he accepted this condition, apparently hoping that his diplomacy would prevent him from having to fight another major war in Europe. Unfortunately for the Emperor, war found France without allies. If the French army had been effective, there would have been no need for alliances. Napoleon was apprehensive, but he accepted war with a heavy heart and the hope that somehow events might turn out all right for him as they often had in the past.

French mobilization was an utter disaster. Men and equipment were hopelessly shipped to the wrong destinations. When the Emperor, in great pain, arrived at Metz with his son, the Prince Imperial, he realized how bad the situation was. The Prussians were expecting a rapid French invasion of South Germany (exactly Napoleon's intent until he saw the chaos at Metz), a move that could have brought Austria and Italy into the war. Bazaine and others, however, favored a defensive posture. The debate on strategy was largely academic, because France lacked the means just then for an invasion of Germany. In Paris the Empress was awaiting news of a French triumph which would allow Napoleon to resume dictatorial and authoritarian rule, making the throne permanently secure for her son. Success in the field, however, was elusive.

Crossing the Rhine above Strasbourg, as Napoleon had hoped, was clearly out of the question. Public opinion in Paris was expecting word of a quick victory, so Napoleon ordered an attack on enemy forces in Saarbrücken. Though successful, it was not part of an integrated offensive and led to nothing. By August 6, three armies invading France had won major victories. Alsace was lost, and in Lorraine the situation deteriorated rapidly, news for which Paris was totally unprepared. Republicans were especially critical, and Ollivier contemplated arresting many of them—including Gambetta, Ferry and Favre. Before he could, however, he was voted out of office. The Empress replaced him with a ministry headed by General Cousin-Montauban, the Count de Palikao.

The members of the new ministry had been selected with no solicitation of the Emperor's views. At the front, he soon lost much of his real authority, granting the title of commander-in-chief to Bazaine on August 12. As French units retreated to Metz several engagements were fought in which the French, enjoying numerical advantage, inflicted heavy losses on the enemy. Bazaine had specific opportunities to turn hard-fought engagements into enemy routs, but instead consistently ordered retreat. For all its logistic confusion, obsolescence and poor leadership, the army fought well. The enormity of the war's loss has obscured view of the occasions when events might easily have led to quite a different outcome.

The Emperor had gone to Chalons to join the army of Marshal MacMahon. There he learned that the Empress desired that he not return to Paris while the army lacked successes. His spirits were low; in acute pain he listened patiently to a lecture from Prince Napoleon on what he should do. Heavy-hearted and taking doses of morphine, he moved on with MacMahon and 130,000 men to Sedan, expecting to move to Bazaine's rescue.

By the time the army was trapped at Sedan, Napoleon's morale had been completely shattered. He deliberately sought death from enemy fire, but when it eluded him he decided that his duty required capitulation in order not to waste 106,000 French lives; 173,000 were to surrender later at Metz. The war continued, but news of the fall of Sedan and the capture of the Emperor emboldened republicans in Paris to demand a republic. The Empress was unable to curb these critics, and the Empire fell on September 4, 1871.

Chapter 4

Life in France
Under the Imperial Regime

Political Life

"Turbulent" is not too strong a word to describe the debates, in the Second Republic's National Assembly, from the 700 spokesmen for various elements in society. After Napoleon's coup and the establishment of another "popular" house, the Legislative Body, the impact of the new regime was unmistakable. The character of political life had changed markedly. Calm acquiescence to government proposals became routine and, before 1859, significant opposition votes were rare.

The membership of the Body assured a minimum of opposition. On February 29, 1852, after the first elections, 253 dedicated adherents to the regime filled all but seven seats. From time to time in the early years a cohesive voting minority would appear over a specific bill, but, lacking ideological unity, it would disintegrate once the particular issue passed. The sessions were too short for extended speechmaking, and since most members supported the government, there was little occasion for it. Except for the Count de Montalembert, a prominent Catholic liberal who had served in the Assembly, no major officials or politicians in the Body had served in previous governments.

From its inception the concerns of the Body were mainly administrative rather than political. It was expected to pass bills rather than to be a forum for a continuous testing or challenging of the government. Like the docile Senate and Council of State, the Legislative Body was designed and constitutionally designated as one of the means by which Napoleon governed. It was *not intended to represent the people,* despite the public's role in electing its membership. For this chamber to become a representative organ, as it had by 1870, was for the Emperor to allow a basic change in its function. The few republicans elected before 1860 were small voices, essentially alone, who had never accepted the formal purpose of the Body as stated in the constitution of 1852. Until the sixties significant dissent was largely stilled.

The supporters of the government who sat in the Body were largely newcomers to public life. They were solidly respectable men of substance in an expanding middle class and had achieved their position by careers of accomplishment in business or the professions. *Parvenu* like the Emperor, their prominence was based on service rather than intrigue. Though defenders and creatures of the regime, they were essentially apolitical, seeing their role exactly as it was defined in the constitution. Their election in large numbers represented a substantial success for the government, which sent circulars to the prefects stressing how desirable it would be in each case to elect a man who "has made his fortune through work, industry, or agriculture, has improved the lot of his workers and has made noble use of his wealth" rather than to entrust bills to mere politicians. The emphasis was on achievement and service, and legislators were merely expected to help in administering the system.

The general public also had become less politically minded. Proscriptions following the coup had effectively assured almost complete silence and conformity. More than 15,000 persons were sentenced to exile (another 9,500 sent to Algeria), while those confined in France numbered over 2,800. There was a literal absence of many persons who would normally be critics. At the same time alert supervision of the press made it particularly difficult to present hostile ideas to the public. The forums of debate had thus been effectively closed and the public expression of opposing views was rare.

Beyond the borders of France the exiles gathered occasionally in small groups to console one another. They represented a number of political factions that retained their identity. Many Orleanists found sympathetic listeners among the aristocracies of Western Europe, but no major government would embark upon action in their behalf. This was amply demonstrated when on January 22, 1852, Louis Napoleon decreed the confiscation of Orleanist estates within France. Several governments reacted with formal diplomatic expressions of concern and shock, but the new Napoleon's domestic authoritarianism went essentially unchallenged.

The republicans in exile were generally in poorer straits than the royalists. Many had problems of maintaining a livelihood, and none had ready access to the councils of power in any country. In addition, they were regarded as particularly suspect and often harassed by the police. Their efforts to propagandize against Louis Napoleon frequently met with suppression, as the French foreign ministry regularly complained whenever hostile pamphlets and newspapers attacked Napoleon. From time to time Napoleon issued pardons to many exiles, and while few of these republicans were won over to the regime, they were silenced. Their audience had dwindled as a result of prosperity and a successful foreign policy (until 1859). In short, republicanism temporarily ceased to be an active, nationwide political force.

Republicans were largely urban intellectuals furtively discussing their plight at informal salons, or young lawyers who struck out at the regime in the courtroom while defending violators of the press law. They quarreled among themselves but enjoyed some local successes in creating an opposition in several cities. A prominent republican's funeral would be the occasion for a gathering which, though quiet, had a distinctly political character—especially the death of Arago in 1853 and of Cavaignac in 1857.

These episodes were, at most, mere hints of a vigorous republican ideology and heritage in France. There were no republican plots of violence against the system, and their political weakness in the early years of the Second Empire was abundantly demonstrated by the elections of 1857. The appearance of "The Five" in the Legislative Body was a reminder more than anything else. In the entire country the opposition attracted only 665,000 votes compared with 5,500,000 for government candidates. There were 2,000,000 abstentions, suggesting a widespread apathy toward politics. The public appeared uninterested in alternatives to Bonapartism.

At the same time that republican and Orleanist voices were being subdued, there was a barrage of publicity for things Napoleonic.

Imperial *N*'s appeared in profusion; parallels with the First Empire were pointed out; in 1858 the publication of Bonaparte's *Correspondance* was started. Bonapartism had its own ideology in the Napoleonic legend, which now was supported vigorously by government auspices.

The regime of Napoleon III was an authoritarianism that was dismantled by fits and starts after 1859. The coup was a use of force that enemies of the Emperor never forgot and continuously recalled for the public during the sixties. After the coup there had been a plebiscite, and it was a major item of Bonapartist propaganda that the public endorsed the end of the Second Republic. Napoleon III's defenders trumpeted the idea that his throne rested on the will of a free people rather than on the principle of heredity common in other nations of Europe. While the public probably did prefer Louis Napoleon to any alternative during most of the period between 1848 and 1870, still his position was morally weakened by efforts of his government to manage elections. The freest election of his career was that of 1848 when he was seeking the presidency. After he was in power, government interference was common in elections, though there was always considerable doubt each time about how much this effected the results. The Emperor's elation at the outcome of the balloting in 1870 betrayed an apprehension that the voters might not be "managed" any longer.

Pressure at the polls centered about the prefects. These appointed officials received specific instructions from the minister of the interior and were expected to assure the success of official candidates when at all possible. During the early years of the Empire the prefects controlled elections in the provinces with marked success. They also influenced a host of lesser appointments as well as the awarding of government contracts and were well enough paid to become the centers of local society, wielding political, economic and social influence.

Paris, however, was quite another story, and to the Emperor's embarrassment the republicans consistently found support in the nation's capital. A unique aspect of Louis Napoleon's success in 1848 was that, unlike most other emerging regimes in French history, his was not forced on the country by Paris but quite the contrary. Indeed, he was never genuinely popular in the city he was to transform; and when the Empire fell, Paris reasserted its leadership in proclaiming the republic.

Despite government pressures, a few veteran republicans from 1848 along with some younger adherents were able to channel local discontent into ballots against the official Bonapartist candidates. The two groups quarreled among themselves, and each regarded the other as impractical. This prevented them from agreeing on candidates and diminished their potential representation in the Legislative Body. Nonetheless, they played on general public antipathy toward the Crimean War, and on a series of local misfortunes: the cholera epidemic of 1853–55 (11,000 deaths in 1854 in Paris); poor harvests between 1853 and 1856; and the 1855–56 floods in the Loire, Rhône and Garonne valleys, which ruined harvests and killed livestock. Agrarian disasters resulted in hardships in the fast-growing cities where the government-sponsored emergency relief was barely a palliative.

The threat of physical violence was not a feature of Napoleon's system. Rather, the government's influence was more subtle. The regime offered the public so-called official candidates, men selected because they were reliable supporters of the Empire. Usually they were outright Bonapartists, although some were local men of prominence with no specific sense of party affiliation. Many Orleanists found that they could support the Empire when its favor could bring them a seat in Paris. Official ballots were sent to all registered voters. These ballots contained the name of the government's candidate, and voting consisted mainly in depositing this ballot at the polls. An uninformed peasantry frequently supported the official candidates without realizing that ballots with other names might be cast. At the polling places there was always some appointee of the government to "assist" the unenlightened, helping them to deposit the "right" ballot. At the local level the idea was deliberately fostered that to oppose the official candidate reflected on one's patriotism and sense of citizenship.

Another arm of the government felt throughout the country was the political police. There was a vague awareness that spies were always close at hand, and candid discussions in public were often in hushèd tones. This characteristic of the regime has been well documented by writers living in that period, who commented frequently about the government's crude surveillance efforts. It also fits the picture of a nineteenth-century totalitarian police state described by some twentieth-century historians. This image, however, must be tempered by a realization that the political police was neither created nor expanded significantly under Napoleon III. Annual funds spent for such activities were far less during the Empire than in 1848, and not much above the average for the years since 1825. Interestingly enough, the attempt to establish a ministry of general police in 1852 was opposed vigorously by the prefects and was abandoned in June of 1853.

The prefects were aided in their task of maintaining order and security by the *Gendarmerie*, which was scattered in small brigades all over France. *Gendarmerie* practices of reporting on police activity directly to the Emperor created apprehensions among the prefects. Other reports to the Emperor, also by-passing the prefects, were sent in regularly by the procureurs general on a wide range of local sentiment and conditions. Thus Napoleon had confidential reports from several points of view from all parts of France. The over-all impression of a spy network was perhaps inevitable, especially since various levels of officials knew others were also making reports. The idea was for the Emperor to acquire accurate information about public opinion, but the techniques he used ensured a reputation of underhanded spying. His method was typical of a man to whom intrigue came naturally.

As the reign wore on, the opportunities for dissidents to criticize and to organize electoral opposition increased. Relaxation of press restrictions made it easier to express discontent, and in the sixties foreign policy failures gave solid topics for malcontents to dwell upon. Typical of Napoleon's dilemma was the Roman Question and his subsequent loss of substantial clerical support as a result of the enormous extension of the Sardinian state. At the same time, by his protection of the Pope in Rome he lost sympathy of those who were anticlerical.

While active opponents of the Empire thus were able to organize progressively stronger opposition votes through 1869, they were not quite the emphatic indictment the republicans claimed. These ballots were, after all, for seats in the Legislative Body; they were not on the viability of the Empire. Too, the opposition was badly fragmented and divided by opportunism. By 1869 the *combined* opposition was significant, but there was never a segment remotely as popular as the regime itself. "The Five" had fallen out in 1864 when Ollivier was prepared to accept the government's compromise of temporary associations for labor rather than outright permanent unions. Thiers and Gambetta vigorously criticized the Empire, but Thiers was a very reluctant convert to republicanism. There were many critical orators but hardly any responsible opposition leaders. At their strongest in 1869, they failed to break Napoleon's grip on the countryside, and urban votes for republicans, Orleanists, democrats, legitimists and others were more than balanced by peasant loyalties. The lower clergy and the agrarian laborers, elements the Emperor had done relatively little for, proved largely impervious to the many fomenters of dissension. France was a nation of factions, and even in 1869 that faction supporting the Emperor remained larger than the others combined.

Imperial Initiatives and Economic Expansion

France enjoyed prosperity during the Second Empire. There were, of course, fluctuations in the economy, but living conditions were generally improved over those of the late forties. This, of course, benefited the regime, especially in the fifties when memories of hardships were still vivid. There was a remarkable expansion of business and economic opportunity. Napoleon had predicted that just such domestic vitality would accompany an imperial system, and when it came to pass he naturally claimed the credit.

The question of how responsible Napoleon III was for the remarkable prosperity during much of his reign is a matter of some debate among historians. Any government after 1848 that could have assured order would probably have been accompanied by rising prosperity. It is true that a number of successful programs during the Empire had been advanced under Louis Philippe. The construction of rail lines is a good example. Napoleon, however, had a conception of his role greater than *only* to maintain order and continue worthwhile programs. There is no doubt that the Emperor believed government had a responsibility to do what it could to encourage economic progress, with special emphasis on improving living conditions for the masses. He claimed that previous governments in France had ruled mainly with the support of the nation's million educated citizens but that his interest was more in the other twenty-nine million. Thus his government would be avowedly dedicated to the plight of the lower classes—though critics have observed that the poverty stricken benefited little while the middle class reaped enormous benefits.

Although the results the Emperor had hoped for did not materialize, his role is clear in bringing the government into the activities of business. At heart he was an ideologue, intensely interested in social questions, a worthy contemporary of Louis Blanc and Proudhon. As a prober of ideas he would have been comfortable in the Frankfurt Assembly. The accident of his birth as a Bonaparte merely added the tradition of militarism and republicanism to a romantic and humanitarian temperament. He accepted the idea of Saint-Simonians that in the environment of the advancing nineteenth century, capitalism had become the new feudalism. The new leaders were men of business acumen—they were, however, to be honored as technicians in the new Bonapartist society in which the lower classes would be protected and enjoy full employment.

With these ideas it is no wonder that he attracted to government service a number of Saint-Simonian disciples. Such men as Michel Chevalier, Prosper Enfantin, the Péreire brothers and Achille Fould were businessmen whose main interests were far removed from politics. They were no more Bonapartists than they had been Orleanists while pursuing their plans under the aegis of Louis Philippe. Prominent in this group and a valuable liaison was Morny, the Emperor's half-brother. As minister of the interior he was in a position to direct imperial activities in business and also to recognize and reward men of competence. It is interesting that while the Emperor promoted the expansion of business, he retained his perspective; he never became victim of its spokesmen and short-range values, as was shown by his affirmation of free trade. In the Cobden-Chevalier treaty he supported this ideology in the face of vigorous opposition by a host of business leaders.

The Second Empire was a golden age for entrepreneurship, as a society that had been fairly stable suddenly began expanding its productive capacity and its horizons. The government's primary role in this lay in its efforts to create new sources of credit. The answer was found in the idea of joint-stock investment companies and in the creation of new banking units, initially supported by reserves in the treasury which had been built up during the reign of Louis Philippe and miraculously not expended during 1848. *La haute banque,* dominated by old families, had remained staunchly Orleanist and, like the Rothschilds, initially revealed a reluctance to support the *parvenu* Emperor. The Bank of France was not properly funded to finance the demands of a burgeoning industry. At best, these existing banks had only dabbled with the idea of the joint-stock company.

Two important new organizations were firmly established in 1852.

In that year a series of land-banks or mortgage banks (*Sociétés de crédit foncier* and *Banques foncières*) were authorized in several French cities. On December 10, 1852, the Paris bank absorbed those in Marseilles and Nevers, becoming the *Crédit Foncier* for France, a new major national financial unit like the Bank of France. Given an initial subsidy of some 10,000,000 francs, it lent 50,000,000 on property within two years. In the sixties its function broadened to the granting of loans to various local units of government. The basic idea of the *Crédit Foncier* had been to provide funds for agriculture and agricultural experimentation, but this particular use never materialized. Instead of agricultural entrepreneurs, enterprising real estate speculators used the funds for property manipulation and profit-making.

A second important institution founded in 1852 was the *Crédit Mobilier*, a joint-stock bank organized by Fould and the Péreire brothers along lines similar to the *Crédit Foncier*. The *Crédit Mobilier* was explicitly intended to provide the cash for large-scale business ventures. Astute businessmen freely used its resources to finance all sorts of major enterprises. Within three years the company's stock had nearly quadrupled in value.

Meanwhile, members of *la haute banque* bought into the new companies and the Bank of France was also able to extend its operations. An unparalleled period of construction took place in France as a direct result of the enormous increase in credit that the Emperor and his advisers had created. This grafting of Saint-Simonian ideas to a Bonapartist regime gave rise to a most appropriate characterization of the Emperor—"Saint-Simon on horseback."

While establishing basic new institutions of credit, the Emperor and his colleagues were also improving the nation's transportation facilities. By the end of 1851 France had slightly over 3,500 kilometers of railway track, managed by eighteen different companies. Most of the rail lines extended radially from Paris, terminating at the channel ports of Dunkirk, Calais, Boulogne, Dieppe and Havre to the north, at Saarbrücken, Strasbourg and Basle in the east, Lyons, Montbrison and Nevers, Chateauroux and Angoulême to the south, and Le Mans and Nantes to the west. Many of these lines had been planned and begun as early as 1842; but by 1848 only 1,900 kilometers were finished. After 1852 work progressed rapidly with about 14,000 additional kilometers completed by 1870. The new lines extended to Brest and Cherbourg in Brittany and Normandy;

and in the south, Bordeaux and Toulouse were now linked with Bayonne, Marseilles and Lyons. Major truck lines connected all important cities and a host of subsidiary lines served the provinces. Links were also established to the major foreign lines where French finance was playing a crucial entrepreneurial role.

The impact of the railroad on the French economy and society can hardly be overstated. Aside from creating employment by their construction, they stimulated businesses whose products could now reach much broader markets. Paris assumed a position of economic dominance, and the provincial centers similarly found their own positions enhanced. Over a decade after the fall of the Empire it was finally obvious that for a vast number of small towns and villages, the coming of the railroad had meant a significant broadening of horizons and opportunities.

Rail construction was only one of the ways in which transportation and communication were improved during the Second Empire. There was also an extensive program of highway development, which, like the railroad, consisted of furthering projects already begun and adding a whole network of secondary routes. At the same time the electric telegraph was being introduced into the major cities of France. First available to the public in 1850, by 1857 it had transmitted over 450,000 messages. The telegraph also strengthened the ascendant position of the leading cities.

The unleashing of credit by paternalistic government decrees had its impact as well on water transportation, an area largely neglected by the regime of Louis Philippe. New maritime companies were founded, and five special transatlantic lines were established after 1857, enhancing the importance of Bordeaux, Le Havre, and Saint-Nazaire. This was the period of the transition from sail to steam in water transport; and while steam-driven tonnage increased some eightfold, the decade after 1848 saw the expansion of sail-driven tonnage by a remarkable 50 per cent. As overseas water transport grew rapidly, within the nation belated efforts were made to extend the network of canals. Apprehensions that railroads would make canals superfluous had delayed these programs until the sixties.

Easier credit allowed such able entrepreneurs as Achille Fould, Paulin Talabot and the Périere brothers to direct vast increases in industrial production and technological advance. In the first decade of the Empire some 70 per cent more machines in 70 per cent more plants produced 70 per cent more horsepower. Coke was rapidly replacing wood in the smelting process, and although coal production doubled between 1850 and 1860, it lagged far behind demand. In the same period manufacturing of cast iron and steel more than doubled.

With growth in both product sophistication and market came the founding of a number of department stores, such as the Bon Marché, La Belle Jardinière, and Printemps, in 1852, 1856 and 1865 respectively. The success of this merchandising innovation in Paris demonstrated that the affluent middle class had been dramatically enlarged.

With the quickening of the economy and the public demanding more of life's amenities, it was only natural that the Bourse should become more prominent—especially since there were so many new companies and the government was becoming closely associated with various commercial enterprises. At the Bourse, the many businessmen immersed in the detailed work of funding serious and well-conceived projects were joined by a horde of speculators. These leeches lent an air of disreputability to dealings at the Bourse.

More serious, perhaps, was the involvement of highly placed government officials. These men invested carefully themselves, taking advantage of their inside knowledge about government decisions, or in many instances they merely "sold" the information. This was especially the case with urban renewal projects, and few in the government were above suspicion. Morny was a major offender in the eyes of many, and Marshal de Saint-Arnaud was suspected of conducting the army during the Crimean War in a way that would enhance his investments. The shadow of corruption fell so broadly on imperial officials that Napoleon, realizing it was a political liability, favored a clamping down on speculators. This never happened, though, and frequent scandals provided republicans during the sixties with material for oratory against the regime. In Paris the prefect's slipshod bookkeeping and irregular floating of loans drew criticism from Jules Ferry that embarrassed the Empire just when it was in need of new funds.

While businessmen and speculators alike were making money, the working class grew larger but did not share commensurately in the new prosperity. Politically it remained suspect because of the June Days and the scattering of uprisings in June, 1849. It was assumed to have radical socialistic views and to be especially susceptible to demagogues. The Emperor saw to it that army units were always ready for action in the industrial centers, the garrisons in Paris and Lyons being the most critical. Two hundred had been killed on the barricades in Lyons in 1849, and plotting against the regime continued there *sub rosa*. As the Empire provided more and more employment opportunities, most of the workers became politically inactive. Nonetheless, the government continued to watch them, collecting regular reports from both confidential and official agents. To aid in this surveillance, each worker was required to have a *livret*, a sort of passport or identity card.

Important questions regarding working hours and wages were settled by local committees or councils whose members were appointive, in which, supposedly, both labor and management were represented. Unfortunately, these failed to serve the workers' interest and often became merely devices to control them—despite Napoleon's explicit directions to managers that laborers be given a fair share of industry's profits. Labor unions and strikes had been forbidden in France since 1791 (the Chapelier Law). With increasing industrialization the agitation for unions became more widespread. The Emperor was sympathetic, but he worried lest they become centers for revolutionary plotting. The government struck a middle course by allowing workers to form temporary coalitions in order to bargain or strike in a particular instance.

As part of the general liberalization of the regime, regular unions were allowed in 1868, making it easier for labor to organize for effective strikes—and there were many strikes in the closing years of the Empire. By 1870 French workers had developed a clear sense of class consciousness, and in the unions they possessed the organization to give substance to their complaints.

Government-sponsored industry and construction was partly designed to reduce unemployment. Napoleon did not push his scheme for relocating workers on barren lands, which he had proposed while at Ham. That plan had been devised to solve the problem of masses of unemployed workers in the cities, but growing industrialization had partly solved the dilemma and Algerian colonization provided another avenue of opportunity. The times and problems had changed, and the Emperor's regime recognized this by making some provisions for old-age pensions and health insurance.

Despite his apprehension about labor's radical tendencies, Napoleon III had done more for workers and for the poor than any French leader since 1800. Union development had been slower than in England, but the French laborer enjoyed the franchise earlier. Social welfare legislation combined with the aggressive promotion of programs for industrial expansion made the lot of the worker in France enviable to much of Europe. The English government did not use its power at this time to promote economic progress, and welfare legislation in Germany was not to begin until 1881. Napoleon had combined free trade with incentives to business, resulting in both continued employment and the social betterment of France and most of her people.

Of the various classes the bourgeoisie experienced the greatest change. They grew tremendously in numbers and in wealth, profiting from the feverish economic activity of the Empire. Their absorption with the challenges of business largely diverted them from political issues and long made their ranks impervious to republican blandishments. They reveled in the advances of modern technology and comforts and in two great expositions showed the world new standards of material progress.

The first World's Fair ever held in France took place in 1855. Special railroad rates and schedules (planned by Prince Napoleon) enabled many from the provinces to attend. Sovereigns from western and central Europe were among some five million visitors who marveled at the advances flowing from machinery and steel. The Emperor was a genial host to this wartime extravaganza of progress. The Exposition of 1867 was an even greater industrial triumph, though the Mexican fiasco was then dampening the Emperor's spirits. This time there was a larger gathering of royalty, and diplomatic maneuvering was a troublesome by-product. As in 1855 the emphasis was on machinery and technical progress, but there was now more of an international flavor.

The 1867 Exposition helped to secure and spread the image of Paris as a tourist mecca abounding in easy pleasures and loose morality, a reputation of remarkable durability. While the hordes of visitors were being impressed by the many formal displays of material progress, their attention was also drawn to Paris itself, where a virtual architectural renaissance had taken place. The city, indeed, was hardly recognizable as that of 1848. Its shape had been altered during a massive program of reconstruction, one of Napoleon's most striking domestic achievements.

Before the Second Empire, Paris had grown haphazardly over the centuries. Dignified structures built during the Renaissance were enmeshed in a veritable warren of winding alleyways and streets. The passion for order and balance associated with Enlightenment architecture and the widespread copying of Versailles had never been applied to the capital. Louis Napoleon had studied plans for the modernization of the city even while preparing for the coup d'état in 1851.

The boldness of the giant renewal project required a supervisor of unusual ingenuity and determination. Such a man was Baron Georges-Eugene Haussmann, a prefect at Bordeaux with a record of efficiency in dealing with socialists. Haussmann was a harsh authoritarian who spoke his mind and ran roughshod over other people's rights. In 1853 he was transferred to the Seine prefecture to undertake the renovation of Paris. With the full support of the Emperor he plunged into his prodigious assignment.

The design for reconstructing the city was nothing less than revolutionary. Broad and straight tree-lined boulevards were to intersect, creating massive squares. This openness gave a sense of light and space to the city, which both contemporaries and generations of visitors since have enjoyed. The Emperor's critics at once attributed the planning of the boulevards to a scheme for making barricades nearly impossible. They noted that small segments of the city could now be sealed off from one another. Artillery could be fired down the boulevards against insurgents and cavalry could be used with telling effect. Under Louis Napoleon, Karl Marx observed, liberty, equality and fraternity had given way to considerations of infantry, cavalry, and artillery. Napoleon was too practical a ruler not to recognize that boulevards would indeed make future calls-to-the-barricades most difficult, but this hardly warranted the criticism that the renovation of the capital was undertaken explicitly for this purpose.

Considerable thought centered on how to lessen or prevent traffic congestion; the answer was found in the creation of open spaces within the city. Consequently the railroad stations and other major public facilities bordered on large squares. Spaces were also deliberately created around existing buildings which were either important or architecturally striking.

The plans for all this open space meant massive condemnation of existing housing. Graft and speculation abounded as the government proved unable to control the financial aspects of the rebuilding. Prices skyrocketed on buildings marked for confiscation so that the government usually paid inflated prices. The money, however, came from government loans which were subscribed to by many of these speculators in property who were amassing wealth at a prodigious rate.

In addition to tearing down buildings to create more space, there was also leveling with a view to rebuilding according to a consistent plan. Buildings of like design went up on a massive scale, resulting in what has often been called a feeling of uninspired uniformity. Combined, however, with the squares and boulevards, the resulting impact was one of dignity and grandeur.

The construction of new housing with sewerage and an adequate water supply within the city (some 40,000 housing units replaced 20,000 destroyed) led to a striking shift in the city's population. Formerly the upper stories were inhabited by workers, while the bourgeoisie lived in the lower and more comfortable quarters. Now all housing within Paris was too expensive for workers and *en masse* they moved to the periphery of the city. With industry also confined to outer areas, the center became solidly bourgeoisie, its businesses being bureaucratic, touristic and professional. The worker now seemed remote to the middle classes, since most daily contact with him had disappeared. Thrown closer together by circumstances, their numbers swelled by a flow of peasants from the countryside, the workers developed more of a sense of identity and solidarity.

The consequences of this relocation are crucial to the understanding of French political and social history since 1880. The center of Paris was given over to pleasure and its pursuits, with the sidewalk café a new feature contributing to lighthearted casualness, while the outer suburbs took on an aspect of grime and poverty. The city formally expanded to include these areas in 1860, and by the end of the Empire, Paris had about doubled its area and increased its population by 40 per cent. An unhealthy and dying city had taken on a core of lasting beauty. It was one product of autocracy that won praise from contemporaries—Louis Blanc was among those applauding the work—and later generations alike. One historian has suggested that anything less than an extended absolutist regime could not have accomplished such an ambitious program.

At the same time similar but smaller-scale renovations were taking place in many of the provincial cities. Construction was at fever pitch in France and the population in major industrial centers increased by percentages ranging from 50 to 300. The middle class was finding an outlet for its energies, and progress (accompanied by graft and speculation) was apparent on every hand. That fewer of the benefits came directly to the lower classes was a drawback, although the changes were so profound that the lives of almost everyone were affected. Living standards had increased enormously. Fashionable spas and seaside resorts became available to the broadening middle class as well as to aristocrats; and while workers hardly enjoyed such vacations, public parks and gardens were in abundance. It was true that rising prices operated to the laborer's disadvantage, but he now lived better and, as Louis Napoleon had recommended at Ham, he had been given expectations.

The Church and the Limits of Intellectual Life

During the Second Empire, Catholicism in France experienced a conservative revival. Though the Church was never as close to the throne as during the reign of Charles X, its resurgence under Napoleon III was pronounced. The Church in France had watched Louis Philippe fall with relative equanimity but was alarmed by the excesses under the Provisional Government. The clergy in 1848 allied with a number of conservatives and Orleanists, including Thiers, who declared that the Church was the only positive foundation for social order. Movements of social Catholicism and clerical democracy appeared to stand for disorder and revolution. The new clerical coalition supported Louis Napoleon as a champion of order, turning against Cavaignac because of his dedicated republicanism with its accompanying inference of public non-clerical education.

Napoleon had a tacit obligation to repay the Church, and for over twenty years his state rendered it favor and francs alike. Universal suffrage had enabled the Church to prove it could deliver the vote through the local clergy's influence over the peasantry. When election results of December, 1848, demonstrated this power in the provinces, Napoleon clearly recognized both his debt and his opportunity. Immediate repayment took the form of the Expedition to Rome in 1849 and an expanded Church role in education, made possible by the Falloux Law of 1850. For these and other deeds the Church supported the coup, permanently abandoning the republic. Mutual favors continued until 1859. After Louis' Italian venture rendered the Papacy more exposed to the forces of nationalism, the Emperor was criticized and occasionally opposed by important clerics. Despite outcry from higher members of the hierarchy, the provincial clergy remained loyal. The stoically conservative local priesthood had its roots in the peasantry and consistently delivered the vote. For this the Church in France continued to receive government favors.

Under the Empire outright monetary benefits for the Church were substantial. In 1852, 39,500,000 francs were budgeted for the Church; by 1868 this figure had risen to 48,000,000 and there were frequent special appropriations. Clerical salaries were increased. Bishops found their income raised from 10,000 to 15,000 francs; archbishops received 20,000 instead of 15,000; cardinals received a 10,000 franc increase in addition to being senators, which brought them another 30,000 francs. The lower clergy received less, but many new offices were created; 1,600 new parishes were established under one guise or another. Government interference in the selection of personnel throughout the hierarchy was at a minimum as Napoleon's regime proved to be a much better friend of the Church than Louis Philippe's.

Besides getting richer, the Church received special exemption from various aspects of Napoleon's authoritarianism. Laws restricting public assembly, for example, were not applied to religious conferences, which met with ever-increasing frequency. Similarly the press regulations did not limit Church publications, and the decree of March 24, 1852, forbidding political societies was adroitly circumvented in the proliferation of lay religious organizations, where a great deal of political discussion occurred.

Most newspapermen were harassed and closely watched by the government, but the Catholic press flourished. Perhaps the best known clerical publication was *L'Univers*, edited by Louis Veuillot. When it broke with the Emperor on the Roman Question in 1859, it was closed down from early 1860 until 1867, its place being taken by the docile *Le Monde*. There were, in addition, many other Catholic papers. By 1862 twenty-five clerical journals served a wide reading public. Of particular importance were *L'Annee Dominicaine*, *Les Annales Franciscaines*, and the Jesuit *Les Etudes Religieuse* (started in 1853, it eventually appeared in every diocese), *L'Almanach du Clergé* and *La France Ecclésiastique*, which merged in 1856, and *Le Moniteur des Paroisses*. Most of these papers were conservative, as liberal Catholics found fewer supporters after 1852. Montalembert grew bitter, and in 1868 Monsignor Dupanloup, Bishop of Orleans, embraced a lonely cause by supporting Le Français, a journal for liberal Catholics.

Conservative Catholicism was enjoying its ascendancy under Napoleon III. Essentially ultramontane and supporting domestic authoritarianism, it had been opposed within clerical ranks by the liberals who were largely Gallican (that is, in favor of administrative independence from papal control of the Church for each nation) and favored parliamentary procedures in national politics. Under the Empire, Gallicanism diminished markedly and Papal authority was strengthened.

The government's role in this movement was curious, considering that Napoleon I did so much to subordinate the Church to state objectives within France. In the field of education the contrast between the policies of the two emperors is perhaps the most striking. The first Napoleon had established the University to supervise all education, thus controlling clerical influence. The Falloux Law of March 15, 1850, was an obvious attack on the authority of the University. The guise of an interest in "freedom in teaching" now allowed more clerical teachers who were "free" of the insidious ideas of Voltaire, which allegedly contaminated all secular teachers. Now the jurisdictions of the University's rectors coincided with the clerical hierarchy, making it easier for Church officials to make their wishes known. Such changes might have been expected under Charles X but were remarkable for a descendant of Napoleon Bonaparte.

While Napoleon III allowed the Church a broader role in education, this indicated his awareness of the need to accommodate the Church rather than his basic views on education. A better indication of these might be gained from the ideas of Victor Duruy, who became minister of public instruction on June 23, 1863. Duruy supported secular education as well as obligatory elementary instruction for both sexes. He struggled against the influence of the Church, which he regarded as not sufficiently nationalistic. He criticized religious instruction in the schools and, in effect, proposed a sort of nullification of the Falloux Law. A few Protestants and Saint-Simonians supported him, but he aroused great hostility among clerical and industrial leaders. Napoleon privately declared himself in support of Duruy's ideas, but in the face of vigorous complaints he advised procrastination in putting these ideas to work. Though consistent opposition prevented full realization of Duruy's hopes, still he was able to expand the educational structure and especially to improve its facilities for advanced study. The issue of the Church in education was put off, to become a major problem for the Third Republic.

As the Church was taking advantage of the Falloux Law, it also experienced a sort of conservative cultural renaissance. In 1852 the Oratory of Jesus Christ, an aged but then decrepit Catholic order, was reorganized and showed a new vitality by taking the lead in arranging conferences to study religion's crucial importance to society. The object was a union between modern thought in science, the arts, letters and Christian doctrine. The gatherings, scenes of intellectual ferment, were duplicated by other Catholic groups. The mood of the movement was a dynamic conservatism which saw a strong Church as the basic guarantee for order and civilization—a point of view that Chateaubriand, de Maistre and de Bonald would have found congenial, but about which a Bonaparte might be expected to have some reservations.

The resurgence of theological discussions resulted in an impressive literature on the vital nature of the Church and its civilizing mission among men. A host of new studies appeared, condemning secularism and exploring the history of the sacramental system and various points of dogma. Thomism now won many adherents since its basic Christian philosophy was closely aligned with the objectives of Church leaders in France.

There was, however, in all of this new study little emphasis on basic documentation and much attention to analysis and faith. As a result the leading Church intellectuals in France were not foremost among the nineteenth-century scholars who were applying new standards of criticism to Biblical scholarship. An exception was Ernest Renan, who combined an earlier training for the priesthood with a skeptical and critical spirit. His *Life of Jesus* (1863) was not his best work but his most sensational. Eminently readable, it presented to a broad audience the latest insights of philology and related work being carried on in Germany. The gist of Renan's startling message was that Christ was an ordinary person, a peasant really. In brilliant language he portrayed a very human person possessing qualities of great moral leadership but no special divinity. This perspective was new for France and marked the start of critical religious writing for that nation. At the moment, however, it brought down the wrath of the clergy. When he repeated his basic views in a lecture at the Collège de France in his capacity as a professor of Hebrew, he was fiercely criticized. It was interpreted as a foray into religion when he was expected to confine his instruction to language and literature. In the face of a clerical storm, the government forced his resignation. Ironically, the problem fell in the jurisdiction of Duruy, who fundamentally opposed Church interference in education.

The regime has been censured for being so responsive to conservative clerical opinion, but it should be recalled too that it was Napoleon III who earlier encouraged Renan in his work; it was Napoleon who sent Renan to the Holy Land to pursue his studies. This experience is credited with tempering Renan's scholarship, adding to it an intensely poetic quality which made his Jesus a real live man. And it was also the Emperor who gave Renan his appointment at the college when he returned. It was a short-lived professorship, but his removal did not end his writing, which continued apace. He also retained his title and its income for two years.

The Renan episode gave rise to a series of special conferences which in turn generated intense conflicts and an extensive polemical literature. The hierarchy remained hostile to the new learning and received government aid in its opposition when necessary. Nonetheless, within the Church a new intellectual ferment had developed which has been overlooked by some historians who have seen only that Renan was dismissed or that Montalembert's liberal ideas had been largely rejected.

Similarly, in the secular realm it is a mistake to infer from Victor Hugo's writing in exile that an active literary and scholarly life could not and did not exist in France. In non-theological historical writing, Victor Duruy was a respected authority on Greece and Rome who drew criticism from conservatives for his preference of Athens over Sparta. It was to Duruy that the Emperor turned for editorial advice on his own study of Julius Caesar. A by-product of Napoleon's work on Caesar was a renewed interest in archaeological work on the early history of Gaul, as well as a concern for other artifacts of the nation's history. The government generously supported restoration of historical sites, such as the rebuilding and renovation of the old city of Carcassonne. Among prominent historians able to write under the Empire was the republican Jules

Michelet, whose pages are still moving to readers a century later. Michelet romanticized the role of the common people in French history and described them in language evoking a passionate pride. De Tocqueville, Thiers and Guizot were able to write under the reign and Fustel de Coulanges began his brilliant career in the latter half of the Empire. Louis Blanc and Edgar Quinet wrote from exile, but Napoleon's early authoritarianism did not prevent scholarly historical writing in France.

Aside from the growing Thomism in the Church, philosophy continued the positivism defined by Auguste Comte before his death in 1857. This new perspective optimistically insisted that scientific data yielded positive if limited knowledge, justifying and stimulating the scientific study of man and society as well as nature. Materialism was a comfortable partner of positivism, and both were naturally attacked by the Church. The early career of Hippolyte Taine spanned the Empire, and his ideas on psychology, history and determinism made him a leading scholar hated in clerical circles. Similarly repugnant to the Church for his rationalism was Emile Littré, a man of prodigious learning who, despite the views of the clergy, was highly regarded among intellectuals and regularly appeared at Princess Mathilde's salon. The ideas of Kant and Hegel were respected in France, and Renan, for one, could be counted among their adherents. Idealism, however, never won a wide following in mid-nineteenth-century France, as here the impact of Auguste Comte proved decisive. The rationalism of Descartes seemed to point French intellectuals in the direction of problems of this world rather than toward metaphysics. Thus the French thinkers settled on social and political problems and their known historic causes; the range of possibilities for serious study of government may be suggested by two names alone, Napoleon III and Proudhon, the imperialist and the anarchist. By mid-century the Romantic movement was well beyond its high-water mark in France, although it still profoundly affected historical writing.

In literature there was a general reaction away from much of Romanticism and toward realism. During the Empire the novel was the ascendant form. Gustave Flaubert was one of the most talented writers in this genre. He found his themes and subjects near at hand rather than in history, the Bible or Greek mythology. *Madame Bovary* was recognizable to every adult because its narrative was a mirror of society. Degradation was recorded, with no exhortation for change. The clergy were often offended, and in the case of Flaubert the Empress personally made sure that the author was speedily brought to trial on grounds that *Madame Bovary* was an offense to public morality and religion. Baudelaire was similarly tried. Both authors received mild condemnations which merely enhanced their reputations and the sale of their works. The favorite at court was the less substantial but more entertaining Prosper Mérimée.

Among the flood of writers during the Empire was Charles Sainte-Beuve, an author who specialized in criticism. Formerly sharing republican sentiments, he became a staunch supporter of the Empire and Napoleon III on the Hobbesian grounds that order was essential and that a bestial savagery was always close by. A friend of Victor Hugo's (and lover of Madame Hugo); he especially admired the work of Renan and Taine. His support of the Emperor seems to have been completely sincere since he admired the objectives of the Saint-Simonians and saw Napoleon as one of them, coining the expression "Saint-Simon on Horseback." Sincere or not, his support of the regime won him a 'senatorship and a regular invitation to Mathilde's salon. Sainte-Beuve authored several books, the most important being *Port-Royal*, a study of Jansenism, but his fame rests on his work as a reviewer of current literature. With Sainte-Beuve, literary criticism came of age as a genre.

The lightheartedness of the new Paris of the Second Empire was exemplified by the musical productions of Jacques Offenbach, a Jew from the Rhineland who accepted both the Catholicism and the mood of his adopted country. His music entertained the Emperor and others without being ponderous; it was vivacious, fresh and exciting. He had caught the temper of his age, but there was more than the beat of the can-can to the Parisian world of music. The French capital had long been a prominent center of opera. The peculiarly French *opéra lyrique* and *opéra bouffe* were flourishing and the Parisian stage was one of Europe's most prominent and demanding.

Romanticism had long dominated music, but by the sixties composers were writing scores that while still romantic, had a clearly national flavor. There was also a trend to realism which Hector Berlioz's work made explicit. Berlioz, regarded by Offenbach as the finest composer of the day, was a great orchestrator, his vast spectacles often overwhelming the audience. In the debate over whether compositions endure because of the music or other factors, he insisted that the quality of musical expression was primary, but nonetheless he was careful that his own music accompany themes taken from literary giants, especially Goethe and Shakespeare.

Along with music, ballet flourished; indeed, this period was a high point in the history of French ballet. Of the leading ballerinas, the most talented was probably Emma Livry, who died of burns following a tragic accident in 1862.

Also on stage were a variety of plays presented by an energetic theater. The younger Alexander Dumas was one of the most successful playwrights, producing light comedies in rapid succession. Farces were also popular; the public was enjoying laughter after having been fed a diet of sober historical dramas. Government censorship was a serious problem but was insufficient to stultify the essential vitality of the theater.

In painting, realism was prominent, with Gustave Courbet almost clinically putting on canvas the world as he saw it. His landscapes and portraits were well received, although much of his work showing the ugliness of poverty was regarded as in bad taste. François Millet and Theodore Rousseau best exemplify the "Barbizon School," a group of painters who portrayed farm life, the forest and the sky—skilled landscape painters trying to capture their subjects in the various moods of nature. Millet was particularly important because of his ability, on canvas, to confer grandeur to very humble subjects. He was roundly criticized by intellectuals in a society not yet ready for such democratic themes. There were a number of active portrait painters, appropriate to the intellectual superficiality of the imperial court. One of the favorites was Franz Winterhalter, who specialized in painting beautiful women. More serious was Hippolyte Flandrin, but his portraits, like those of many other court painters, reveal little of the subject beyond a visual impression. It was realism at a low level, but from his brush came the best-known portrait of Napoleon III.

During the Second Empire scientific study showed particular vitality. The fruits of applied science were, of course, available for all to see at the expositions. The Emperor was interested in scientific progress and personally provided assistance for Louis Pasteur. After the Empire had fallen, Pasteur declared that historians would eventually recognize Napoleon III's reign as "among the most glorious in our history."

Pasteur's emotional judgment clearly erred on the optimistic side, especially as far as intellectual freedom was concerned. Public forums were scarce for ideas that ran counter to established conservative clerical opinion. Truly free and open criticism of the regime was also severely limited. However, though the regime was authoritarian, significant intellectual activity was possible and scholarly achievements of a high order occurred during the Second Empire. If some intellectuals pursued their literary work in exile, it was because of their political orientation rather than the substance of their work per se.

Chapter 5

The Emperor and His Empire in the Mirror of History

Sedan, like Waterloo, signalled the end of a Napoleonic regime. A second great battle with a Bonaparte at the front again seared the very core of French national consciousness. With dazzling swiftness Napoleon III was deposed, the enormous accomplishments of two decades overbalanced by failure in war.

The Second Empire was over. Historians, studying this period of French history, discovered that however they presented their data, controversy still surrounded the Emperor, making interpretation difficult and final judgments elusive. To this day each student of the period must decide on largely intuitive grounds whether or not the Emperor possessed real ability, whether or not Napoleon intentionally caused a whole series of basic changes in France. It may be cogently argued that his reign merely coincided with a host of dynamic forces which in some cases he was reluctantly forced to accept. Was he a maker, spectator or victim of circumstances? History might be cyclical, and perhaps vast dialectics are being worked out; but unfortunately, whatever the pattern of history, the known facts are insufficient to dispel lingering uncertainties regarding Napoleon III's capacities, intentions and proper place in history.

Louis Napoleon lived in the shadow of the Napoleonic legend—

the romantic blending of fact and fiction which Bonapartists pretended was a just portrayal of history. He proved that this legacy was potent enough to launch a restoration of Empire, and his new regime lasted longer than its illustrious model. It never managed, however, to acquire similar glory, and it spawned no successful legend of its own.

The absence of a similarly distorting legend about the Second Empire did not mean that it could be more easily evaluated or understood. Since the Third Republic had been born at the expense of Napoleon III, the Second Empire was publicized after 1870 as the grossest type of corrupt and incompetent authoritarianism, an interpretation well-established earlier in the writing of Alexander Kinglake and Victor Hugo. The vision of Napoleon meddling in overseas ventures to distract attention from his foul and criminal regime in France is explicit in the first volume (1863) of Kinglake's study *The Invasion of the Crimea*. Similar sentiments, more emotional and wide-ranging, appeared in Hugo's *Napoléon le Petit* (1852), a diatribe reflecting little credit to its brilliant author.

These views were largely unrefuted for many years, except for an apologetic, family-approved biography by Blanchard Jerrold, a four-volume work published between 1874 and 1882. Late in the nineteenth century the standards of scientific history became widely accepted. In France scholars of the Ernest Lavisse generation narrated events which "spoke for themselves." When they followed the new rules, writing history "exactly as it happened," what conveniently emerged was a comfortable, republican, middle-class orientation toward the Second Empire. The scientific approach eliminated rank emotionalism but left nearly intact the basic republican critique of Napoleon III.

After Napoleon Bonaparte's death in 1821, a flurry of emotional "histories," both favorable and unfavorable, appeared. But, in time, the objective investigator had solid data to work with, including the valuable *Correspondance de Napoléon Ier*, thirty-two volumes, published between 1858 and 1870 by the order of Napoleon III. No such massive body of documents regarding Napoleon III was ever presented to the public.

During the Commune some important records were destroyed; but most important, the Emperor was not a prolific correspondent, and he kept no running diary or journal. Napoleon III has remained an elusive character for historians because of this scarcity of candid material and because his penchant for listening respectfully to the ideas of others allowed them to believe he agreed, giving rise to wide contradictions regarding his objectives. Since the careers of many of the Emperor's associates can be more satisfactorily documented, study of these secondary figures is now one of the most fruitful avenues open for researchers. We need to see Napoleon III from the perspectives of more of his prominent contemporaries. This will tell us more of just what happened and perhaps yield some better clues on why. Investigation of more of the Empire's social programs will illuminate imperial policy. The likelihood is that the Emperor, rather than some minister or the Empress, made the decisions on most major questions. His frequent procrastination had its deadening effect on events and suggests his central responsibility. To get a true picture of "what happened" we need to know on various issues why he decided as he did, when he did. This information remains for historians in the category of unfinished business.

The easier but much less reliable alternative to a search for sounder judgments is to follow the opinions of Napoleon III's contemporaries. In this case, however, the biases of Hugo, Kinglake and Ollivier are well known. Valuable as their narratives are for the historian, so much of their interpretations have been widely and uncritically accepted that scholars interested in the Empire have a special obligation to get closer to the Emperor's motives and perspectives.

The first objective study of Louis Napoleon and the Second Empire may be found in two books by F. A. Simpson, *The Rise of Louis Napoleon* (1909) and *Louis Napoleon and the Recovery of France, 1848–1856* (1923). The portrayal is essentially favorable and rests on a far wider study of contemporary witnesses than any previous accounts. Simpson's work, in fact, may be credited with starting a whole series of revisionist studies, becoming ever more partial to Napoleon and culminating with Albert Guérard's *Napoleon III* (1943) which was so laudatory, almost emotionally so, that it spurred vigorous reactions. The urge to counter the bias of earlier writings may have gone too far, but as a result later works have been more careful and more solidly based. Gordon Wright's discussion of the Second Empire in his *France in Modern Times* (1960) is a brilliant example of fair evaluation and penetrating insight. Though in this case judgment weighs more heavily on the negative side, the pros and cons of men and issues are judiciously stated.

The twentieth century's own problems have suggested interesting new perspectives. J. Salwyn Schapiro's *Liberalism and the Challenge of Fascism* (1949) presented Louis Napoleon and his techniques as an historical forerunner of the fascism of Mussolini and Hitler.

The League of Nations provided the point of departure for yet another view of Napoleon III. Robert Sencourt, in *Napoleon III: The Modern Emperor* (1933), saw Napoleon III as a man ahead of his time in his emphasis on international congresses to anticipate and settle problems.

In the wake of Sencourt's book, many writers noted that Napoleon took seriously the problems of the continent as a whole, perhaps losing sight of some essential French interests in the process. An episode that took place on February 21, 1863, is most suggestive. On that day Eugénie showed the Austrian ambassador a map indicating a more rational drawing of European boundaries. He was amazed at both the candor of the Empress and the new pattern of states. He had known the Emperor for some time, but his shock indicated how little prominent statesmen were aware of Napoleon's ideas about nationalities and ethnically unified states within natural frontiers. The map presumed an independent Poland at the expense of Russia and Prussia. They were to be more than adequately compensated however. Russia was to gain most of Asia Minor and Prussia would make significant gains in North Germany. Venetia would go to Italy, Austria being compensated with Silesia and gains in the Balkans. The Ottoman Empire was gone and the Greeks possessed Constantinople. France had gained the left bank of the Rhine, with the dispossessed German princes perhaps setting themselves up in South America, following the current example of Maximilian in Mexico.

Were all these changes merely a scheme for France to get the left bank? In a completed Italy, a free Poland and an enlarged Prussia in Germany, there was a frank recognition of nationalism and a minimizing of historic causes for war. Napoleon III was both a nationalist and a good European, European in a sense that Bismarck neither was nor would have understood. Napoleon's foreign policy proved disastrous for France, and yet on the question of nationalism his instincts were correct. In both foreign and domestic affairs he deliberately brought intrigue or its appearance into situations where it was unnecessary, so that he appeared to be Machiavellian. However, he lacked the hardness of a real Machiavellian ruler, for inwardly he was sensitive, friendly and gentle.

This man who was so ahead of his time also had the ideals of the enlightened despot in his makeup. Merged with Saint-Simonian theory, it was virtually inevitable that his regime would supervise vast domestic changes. A measure of the success of social adjustments during the Empire was a significant drop in the crime rate. There may have been vast profiteering and pandering to the middle class, but a thoroughgoing economic transition was being carried out. Least affected were the peasants; but after receiving the franchise in 1848, they were voting, literacy was on the rise and new transportation facilities assured further changes.

Politically, Napoleon was moving in the right direction in liberalizing the Empire; but it all looked so forced that until the very end he received little credit for even having good intentions. Had he been harsher and as despotic as his opponents charged, he might have slowed the liberalization process. As it was, he resorted to expedients, largely because he really had no planned program. Though he claimed that the Napoleonic legend constituted a whole program, it did not provide guidance for him once he had acquired power.

In the later years when he was more and more in pain and agony, the daily control of affairs slipped from his hands. His imperial structure had not attracted men of unusual ability to government service, as the First Empire had. If he had found a great minister, a Colbert or a Richelieu, it might have been different; but he had only his fellow aging conspirators and a horde of opportunists, while Orleanist, legitimist and republican zealots waited for him to falter. He failed also to raise a new generation of leaders; yet, when he judged that the moment was appropriate, he was wise enough to yield major segments of his power rather than to insist stubbornly on continuing with Bonapartist cronies. He had given France a constitutional monarchy. There was ministerial responsibility to a lower chamber, elected by universal manhood suffrage, all under the benign guidance of a famous dynasty. Like his observation about his uncle, he could claim to have closed "the gulf of revolutions." And he crowned the edifice with liberty.

Sedan ended the Emperor's active career but he lived for two more years. After six months' detention by the Prussians, he was allowed to join Eugénie and his son in England. There his health seemed to improve and he renewed many old acquaintances.

He also kept up on news from Paris, taking particular interest in the issues separating Orleanists, legitimists and republicans. Almost instinctively he began to speculate and then to plot a return to France—yet another return from Elba. Late in 1872, however, the acute pains associated with kidney stones returned. He had long disregarded medical advice, but now he consented to a series of three operations. On January 7, 1873, he died, failing to recover from the second operation.

With the death of Napoleon III, Bonapartism had run its course. There were still a few reflexive stirrings in France, but no individual appeared who could effectively organize a new movement. The Prince Imperial was killed in 1879, fighting for Britain in the Zulu War. The Empress Eugénie lived with her memories until 1920. She was delighted to see France victorious in a war of revenge to recover Alsace and Lorraine, the scenes of the military disaster that ended the Empire.

A Note on the Literature

This book has tried to present a fair view of the career of Louis Napoleon. While sympathetic to the man, the author attempted to note his shortcomings and mistakes in policy. He also hopes that readers may realize from this brief account the importance of the reign for the history of France and for the history of Europe. At the same time the difficulty of making confident judgments about Napoleon III should be clear.

In Chapter 5 reference has been made to several books about the Empire and to some of the differing points of view on the Emperor. To expand one's knowledge of Napoleon III and his reign the works cited should be carefully explored. In addition there are dozens of other titles in English alone. In French, of course, there are many more, besides an extensive periodical literature. Guides to much of this material may be found in two excellent articles: Robert Schnerb, "Napoleon III and the Second French Empire," *Journal of Modern History*, VIII, 3 (September 1936), and Alan B. Spitzer, "The Good Napoleon III," *French Historical Studies*, II, 3 (Spring 1952). Two works having bibliographical essays are Brison D. Gooch, *Napoleon III: Man of Destiny, Enlightened Statesman or Proto-Fascist?* (1963), and Samuel M. Osgood, *Napoleon III: Buffoon, Modern Dictator, or Sphinx?* (1963). Both of these booklets contain excerpts from major studies, arranged to make clear the variety of interpretations about Napoleon. Information about much of the literature exists in bibliographies in the major studies on the Empire. Many general histories of France deal effectively with the Second Empire and several cooperative works, such as the *Cambridge Modern History*, are also available. Among English titles carried by most libraries, the following represent a cross section:

René Arnaud, *The Second Republic and Napoleon III*, 1930.
Octave Aubry, *The Second Empire*, 1940.

Nancy N. Barker, *Distaff Diplomacy: The Empress Eugénie and the Foreign Policy of the Second Empire*, 1967.

Erna Barschak, *The Innocent Empress*, 1943.

Lynn M. Case, *French Opinion on War and Diplomacy During the Second Empire*, 1954.

Rondo Cameron, *France and the Economic Development of Europe, 1800–1914*, 1961.

Maristan Chapman, *Imperial Brother: The Life of the Duc de Morny*, 1931.

J. M. and Brian Chapman, *The Life and Times of Baron Haussmann*, 1958.

D. G. Charlton, *Positivist Thought in France During the Second Empire*, 1959.

Thomas A. B. Corley, *Democratic Despot: A Life of Napoleon III*, 1961.

Egon Caesar Corti, *Maximilian and Charlotte in Mexico*, 2 vols., 1928.

Augustin Filon, *Recollection of the Empress Eugénie*, 1921.

H. A. L. Fisher, *Bonapartism*, 1914.

Willard A. Fletcher, *The Mission of Vincent Benedetti to Berlin, 1864–1870*, 1965.

Brison D. Gooch, *The New Bonapartist Generals in the Crimean War*, 1959.

George Peabody Gooch, *The Second Empire*, 1960.

Philip Guedalla, *Second Empire: Bonapartism, the Prince, the President, the Emperor*, 1922.

Albert Guérard, *Reflections on the Napoleonic Legend*, 1924.

Charles W. Hallberg, *Franz Joseph and Napoleon III, 1852–1864*, 1955.

Michael Howard, *The Franco-Prussian War*, 1961.

Harold Kurtz, *The Empress Eugénie, 1826–1920*, 1964.

Robert H. Lord, *The Origins of the War of 1870*, 1924.

Karl Marx, *The Eighteenth Brumaire of Louis Bonaparte*, 1852, 1926.

Simone André Maurois, *Miss Howard and the Emperor*, 1957.

Hermann Oncken, *Napoleon III and the Rhine*, 1912.

Franklin C. Palm, *England and Napoleon III*, 1948.

Howard C. Payne, *The Police State of Louis Napoleon Bonaparte, 1851-1860*, 1966.

David H. Pinkney, *Napoleon III and the Rebuilding of Paris*, 1958.

E. Ann Pottinger, *Napoleon III and the German Crisis, 1865–1866*, 1966.

E. A. Rheinhard, *Napoleon and Eugénie: The Tragi-comedy of an Empire*, 1931.

Imbert de Saint–Amand, *Napoleon III and His Court*, 1898.

Robert Sencourt, *The Life of the Empress Eugénie*, 1931.

Nassau W. Senior, *Conversations with M. Thiers, M. Guizot, and other Distinguished Persons During the Second Empire*, 1878.

Lawrence D. Steefel, *Bismarck, the Hohenzollern Candidacy, and the Origins of the Franco German War of 1870*, 1962.

J. M. Thompson, *Louis Napoleon and the Second Empire*, 1955.

Frederick A. Wellesley, ed., *The Paris Embassy During the Second Empire*, 1928.

Roger Williams, *Gaslight and Shadow: The World of Napoleon III*, 1957.

Theodore Zeldin, *The Political System of Napoleon III*, 1958.

Index

Printed in U.S.A.